THE ROBERT AUDY METHOD

JAZZ DANCING

HOW TO TEACH YOURSELF

ROBERT AUDY

PHOTOGRAPHY BY
NEIL SELKIRK

VINTAGE BOOKS
A DIVISION OF RANDOM HOUSE, INC.
NEW YORK

A Vintage Original, June 1978
First Edition
Copyright © 1978 by Robert Audy

Grateful acknowledgment is made to the following for permission to reprint previously published material:
Random House, Inc.: Excerpt from *Tap Dancing: How to Teach Yourself to Tap* by Robert Audy. Copyright © 1976 by Robert Audy.

Twentieth Century Music Corporation: Lyrics from "Ease On Down the Road" by Charlie Smalls. © 1974, 1975, 1977 by Fox Fanfare Music, Inc. All rights reserved.

Library of Congress Cataloging in Publication Data

Audy, Robert.
  Jazz dancing.

  1. Jazz dance.   I.   Title.
GV1753.A9   793.3'2   77-76565
ISBN 0-394-72356-2

Manufactured in the United States of America
2 3 4 5 6 7 8 9
First Edition

Design: Robert Aulicino

CONTENTS

MUSICAL TERMS AND COUNTING STEPS

Here are some basic musical terms and notations you should understand before proceeding with this book.

Measure:
A portion of music enclosed between two lines known as bars. Music is divided into measures, each containing a number of beats. Measures are separated by vertical bar lines, which should not be confused with the ballet bar you will hold on to later during your exercises.

Rhythm:
Within a measure of music, strong and weak beats, or heavily and lightly accented beats, are combined. Rhythm is the regular recurrence of accent, or beats, in music. The steps you will be learning are constructed around the various rhythms found within measures of music.

Tempo:
The rate of speed with which music is played. You will be using different tempos in the work you are about to do. Each exercise includes instructions about the tempo to which you should dance. You can refer to the list I've compiled in the back of the book to get an idea of the kind of music that has the various tempos called for. To get the feeling of the tempo of a piece of music, play some of your favorite songs on the phonograph or radio, and clap your hands to the beat. You may think that you don't understand anything about tempo, but your body does. If you just allow yourself the freedom of clapping your hands as you feel you should, you will find that you will be clapping in time with the music, and will therefore know what the tempo is.

When I talk about "beat," I mean the pulsation of time. There is always an equal amount of time between each pulsation or beat. To understand "beat," do the following exercises:

1) Sit at a table and count from 1 to 8. Hit your finger against the table on each count, being sure to keep an equal amount of time between each drop of the finger.
2) Do the same exercise more quickly and then more slowly, but be sure that you are always dealing in blocks of beats that go up to 8.
3) Now take a piece of music—for example, Stevie Wonder's "Isn't She Lovely?"—and instead of tapping your finger, clap your hands on each beat as you did in the exercise on tempo.

You will need to know how to count to the music so that you can do the steps and combinations at the right moment in each song. Generally speaking, steps in jazz are counted from 1 to 8 (i.e., 1, 2, 3, 4, 5, 6, 7, 8). To understand this, simply walk forward and count as follows: step on right foot, saying "one"; step on left foot, saying "two"; step on right foot, saying "three"; step on left foot, saying "four"; and so on, until you reach eight. (Incidentally, this will be the first walk you will be doing in the chapter on jazz walks.) Sounds that come between beats are counted "and." To understand this, do the following exercise:

First step right on right foot, saying "one"; then cross left foot in back of right, saying "two"; step on right again, saying "three"; then step left foot to left, saying "four." Now vary the exercise this way: step right, saying "one"; quickly cross left in back of right, saying "and"; then quickly step right foot to the right again, saying "two"; then step left foot to left, saying "three"; quickly cross right foot in back of left, saying "and"; step left foot to left, saying "four." In effect, by using the half-beats between the first and second beats and the third and fourth beats, you have done six steps in the time it took you to do four steps before. In the exercises, if you should do a step on "one," a (1) will follow the instructions; if you should do it on "and," a (&) will follow the instructions, and so on.

EQUIPMENT

The following dance-supply stores will be able to provide you with the necessary accessories for your jazz lessons. You may order them directly, or you may write to them and ask for the names of their local distributors.

Capezio   Phone: (212)245-2130
755 Seventh Avenue (betw. 49th & 50th Sts.)
New York, New York 10019

Herbet Dancewear   Phone: (212)677-7606
902 Broadway (betw. 20th & 21st Sts.)
New York, New York 10010

Selva & Sons   Phone: (212)586-5140
1776 Broadway (at 57th St.)
New York, New York 10019

During practice of your jazz lessons, I suggest the following: for women, a leotard and tights, or something loose-fitting in which you can move freely and swing your legs. For men, loose-fitting pants and a sweat shirt in which you have freedom of movement and do not feel confined. I recommend ballet shoes or sneakers as footwear for beginning jazz lessons, but you can buy a special jazz shoe through the above dealers if you really want the feel of jazz dancing. You may also dance in your bare feet for the bar isolations and floor stretches.

Prices on shoes vary. Ballet shoes run $7 and up, and jazz shoes cost about $16.

RECORDS

As I mentioned earlier, at the back of the book you will find a listing of many records appropriate for jazz dancing. Listings are categorized in the following manner — Slow tempo, Medium tempo, Fast tempo, Bounce, Percussion and so on. (You will note that I tell you which category of music is best suited for each exercise.) Once you are familiar with the various tempos, you may then choose other records that fit into the necessary tempo for that particular exercise or step.

HOW TO USE THIS BOOK

You should be sure that your body is completely warmed up before you do the combinations. First read the chapter on "Good Posture." Then proceed with the bar work and the stretches. You don't necessarily have to do all the bar work or stretches during the course of one practice session; however, try to choose a couple of exercises from each section each time you work so that your body has a chance to get used to the movement. Your rate of development will obviously depend upon how much time you can practice, but you should be sure not to do more than your body is capable of on any given day. You may find that your muscles will begin to feel sore after a day or two of this work. The best thing to do is to take a hot bath to keep those muscles loose, then continue to work the next day so that eventually the muscles will stretch and stop hurting. If you don't use those muscles because they are sore, they will only go back to their original state of disuse, and when you try the exercise later you will experience the same problem. (You should move through the book at a rate with which you are comfortable — never straining beyond your ability.) Please also keep in mind that this book provides only the fundamentals of a beginner's introduction to jazz dancing. Most of all, enjoy it! Not only can jazz exercise the body and keep it in tone, but its exercises and techniques can also be used in social and/or discotheque dancing. Jazz should never be a chore; rather, you should think of it as a way to help you release your inner feelings through self-expression and to have fun.

GOOD POSTURE

Before starting any of the warm-up exercises, you should think about posture, since good posture will enable you to keep your balance without holding on to anything.

You were probably told as a child that if you pushed your shoulders back and your chest forward, then you would have good posture. This is not the case — at least not in dancing. It is important, instead, that you hold your body in a *good line*: rather than arching your back and sticking out your buttocks, you should keep your buttocks and shoulders in a straight line. The idea is to make your body flexible — not rigid. By following the instructions outlined below for achieving a good line, you will find strength in your body that will let you really use your legs. The strength, as you will learn, is in the lower abdomen and lower back, and if you develop that area, you will be able to move your entire body with ease and fluidity.

Good posture involves lining up the pelvis and the shoulders with each other. The line from the top of the head to the bottom of the spine should be straight. The shoulders should be relaxed and down. Common faults of beginning dance students are the tensing of the neck and shoulders, the bringing of the head too far forward or back, and the placing of the pelvis incorrectly — either arching the back or pushing the pelvis too far forward. Watch yourself in the mirror as you practice these methods of attaining this line.

First, find the pubic bone — the bone right above the pubic area. Now find the sternum, or breastbone — the thin, flat structure of bone and cartilage to which most of the ribs are attached in the front of the chest. To find the sternum, take the second and third fingers of both hands and place them on the bottom of the ribs. Then move these fingers toward the center of the body, and you will feel a hollow in the middle. Once you find the hollow, take all your fingers away except the index finger of one hand and trace the finger upward toward the center of the chest. At the top of the hollow is the sternum, or breastbone. Now think of an imaginary string drawn taut from the pubic bone to the breastbone. This will bring the buttocks under and place the pelvis in the correct position. Remember to keep the natural curve of the lower spine intact.

When you are standing correctly, your pelvis and shoulders line up with each other.

Next, find the pelvic bones on both sides of the body by placing the hands on the hips, with the thumbs behind and the rest of the fingers in front. The bones that you feel with the fingers in front are the pelvic bones. Once you have found the pelvic bones, try to line them up with the bottom of the ribs. Be sure you don't move the ribs forward or back, but keep them in their natural position while placing the pelvic bones in line with them. This will also bring the buttocks under and place the pelvis in the correct position.

Now that you have a good posture, you can go on with the warm-up exercises. Remember to keep this posture throughout all these exercises. It will take a good deal of concentration, but it will give you the strength you need.

Be sure you don't arch your back,
tense your shoulders and neck,
or bring your head too far forward.

Don't push your pelvis forward either.

BAR WARM-UPS

Dance classes generally begin at the bar, a hand-rail placed around the dance studio's walls at hip height. However, since you are not in a dance studio, you can use the back of a sturdy chair to help you maintain your balance. Refer to these illustrations so that you will know where to hold your arms and place your feet.

First Position Parallel

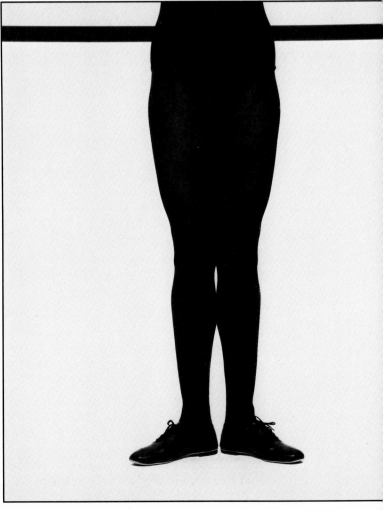

First position Turned Out/Modified "V" Position

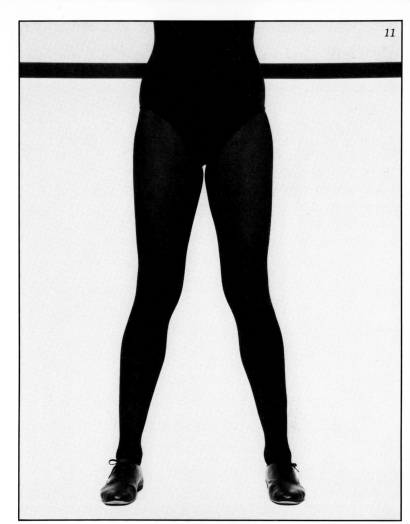

Second Position Parallel

Second Position Turned Out/"V" Position

Arms Overhead

Arms Hanging
Loosely at Sides

Arms in Second Position/
Extended to Sides

Arms in Diamond Shape

EXERCISES

To start the exercises place your left hand on the chair back.

A *plié* (plee-ay) is a bend; in this case, a bending of the knee or knees. This exercise makes the joints and muscles soft and pliable, stretches the Achilles tendon, and develops a sense of balance. There are two types of *pliés*—a *grand plié* (grahn plee-ay), which is a full bending of the knees, and a *demi-plié* (deh-mee plee-ay), which is a half-bending of the knees. *Demi-pliés* are done without lifting the heels from the ground.

Exercise I *Demi-plié* Feet are in first position parallel; right arm out to the side in second position. Do a slow half knee-bend counting to four; then straighten the knees to four more counts. As you are going down into the bend and coming up, be sure that your knees don't fall out to the sides or into the center, but are placed just over the toes. Keep your heels on the floor. Repeat this exercise three more times, remembering to take four counts going down and four counts straightening back up.

Exercise II *Demi-plié* Feet are in second position parallel; right arm out to the side in second position. *Demi-plié*, remembering to keep the knees over the toes and the heels on the floor. Bend the knees, counting to four; straighten the knees to four more counts. Repeat this an additional three times, taking four counts to bend and four counts to straighten your knees.

A *relevé* (rehl-vay) is a raising of the body from the flat feet to the balls of the feet.

Demi-plié, second position:
Bend your knees, remembering to keep your knees
over your toes and your heels on the floor.

Exercise III *Relevé* Feet are in first position parallel; right arm out to the side in second position. Raise your body onto the balls of your feet counting to four; now lower your heels to the floor to four more counts. As you *relevé*, be sure your weight is forward over your toes. Repeat this exercise an additional three times, taking four counts to rise on the balls of the feet and four counts to lower the heels.

Relevé, first position:
Raise your body onto the balls of your feet.

Exercise IV *Relevé* Feet are in second position parallel; right arm out to the side in second position. Raise both body onto the balls of your feet to four counts; now lower heels to the floor to four more counts. Remember to keep the weight forward over the toes. Repeat this exercise an additional three times, taking four counts to raise the heels and four counts to lower them.

Now repeat all the above exercises with the right hand on the chair back so that you get the feeling of using both sides of the body.

Exercise V *Foot and Leg Exercise* This exercise works the calf muscles and the arches of the feet, while stretching the Achilles tendon and hamstring muscles.

Place your left hand on the bar. Put your feet in first position (modified "V"), being sure your body and hips are placed forward, and hold your right arm to the side in second position. Stretch out your right foot while sliding it forward from first position to the front without lifting it off the ground, being sure both knees are straight (1); when the foot is stretched out as far as is comfortable, flex your foot by pointing your toes toward the ceiling while lifting your foot off the floor (2); now return toes to the floor, stretching them once again (3); then bring foot back to first position again (4). Now repeat this once more to the front (5, 6, 7, 8). Now do the same exercise, but instead of stretching the foot to the front, go out to the side. Stretch the right foot to the right side, making sure to keep it on the same line as the other foot—not at an angle to the front or the back—so the right hip is not thrown out of line. Just slide it to the right side without lifting it off the ground, keeping both knees straight (1); when the foot is stretched out as far as is comfortable, then flex the foot (2); now return toes to their stretched position (3); then bring foot back to first position (4). Repeat again to the side—stretch (5); flex (6); down (7) and back to first (8). Now repeat the entire exercise to the back. Stretch right foot in back of you by again sliding the foot without lifting it off the floor (1). Let the big toe rest on the floor, as far back as is comfortable, being careful not to put your weight on the toe; now raise the foot off the floor and flex it (2); then stretch it (3); and bring it back to the original position (4). Remember to keep your hips facing front. Repeat again to the back (5, 6, 7, 8). Now repeat to the side twice. Then turn to the other side, right hand on the bar, and *repeat* entire exercise with left foot. Do it two times to the front; two times to the side; two times to the back; two times to the side, using eight counts for each.

Foot and Leg Exercise:
After you've stretched your foot forward, flex your foot while lifting it off the floor.

Exercise VI *Foot Brushes* Place your left hand on the bar. Place your feet in the modified "V" position, and your right arm out to the side in second position. Stretch the right foot forward in front of your body, by sliding the foot forward and then brushing it off the floor about 3 inches (1); then flex the foot by bending the toes upward (2); then bring the foot back to the stretched brush position while it is still off the floor (3); then bring it back to the original position by bringing the toes down to the floor and sliding the foot back (4). Repeat this again to the front (5, 6, 7, 8). Now do the exercise to the side. Slide the right foot out to the side and brush it 3 inches off the floor (1); flex the foot (2); bring it back to the stretched position (3); return foot to original position by touching toes to floor and then sliding the foot back to the starting position (4). Repeat again to the side (5, 6, 7, 8). Now do this exercise to the back. Slide the right foot back on the big toe and then brush it up 3 inches off the floor (1); flex the foot (2); return the foot to the stretched position (3); bring

the foot back to the original position (4). Repeat again to the back (5, 6, 7, 8) and then two more times to the side (1, 2, 3, 4, 5, 6, 7, 8). Turn to the other side, place your right hand on the bar, and repeat the entire exercise with the left foot.

Slide your right foot forward and then brush it off the floor about 3 inches.

18

Exercise VII *Calf Stretches* Stand with your back straight, facing the bar. Place both hands on the bar. Your left foot should be close to the bar and your right foot should be about 2 feet in back of the left. Knees are straight; therefore, only the ball of the back foot will be on the floor. Now start to bend the left knee as you put the right heel down on the floor (1, 2); straighten left knee and bring right heel off floor (3, 4); again bend left knee, putting right heel down (5, 6); straighten left knee, bringing right heel up (7, 8). Bend left knee and put right heel down (1, 2); now straighten left leg and bring right foot off the floor and bring right knee up so that right thigh is parallel to the ceiling and right toe is pointing toward the floor (3, 4); lower right foot to floor and put your weight on it (5, 6); bring left foot off the floor and bring left knee up so that left thigh is parallel to the ceiling and left toe is pointing toward the

Start the calf stretches with your left foot close to the bar and your right foot about 2 feet in back.

floor (7); place ball of left foot about 2 feet in back of right foot (8). Begin exercise again. Remember: Both knees are now straight, and the ball of the left foot is on the floor. Bend right knee and put left heel down (1, 2); straighten right knee and bring left heel up (3, 4); bend right knee and put left heel down (5, 6); straighten right knee, bringing left heel up (7, 8); bend right knee and put left heel down (1, 2); straighten right leg and bring left foot off the floor, bringing left knee up so that left thigh is parallel to the ceiling and left toe is pointing toward floor (3, 4); lower left foot to floor and put your weight on it (5, 6); bring right foot off the floor and bring right knee up so that right thigh is parallel to the ceiling and right toe is pointing toward the floor (7); place ball of right foot about 2 feet in back of left foot (8). Repeat the entire exercise again—once with the right foot in back and once with the left in back.

Bend your left knee while putting your right heel down on the floor.

Exercise VIII *Leg Stroke Exercise* Place your feet in the modified "V" position and your left hand on the bar. Your right arm is out to the side in second position. Concentrate on the strength of your stomach muscles, remembering to pull your stomach into your spine, and your spine into your stomach. Using these muscles to keep your balance, bring the heel of your right foot off the floor and point your toes. Now slide the toes of your right foot up the side of your left leg until the toes come just below the left knee or wherever you can comfortably stop without turning in the knee (1, 2, 3, 4); lower the right foot, sliding your right toes down your left leg (5, 6, 7, 8). If you lower the foot correctly, the toes should touch the ground first, then the sole of the foot, and lastly the heel. There are a couple of things to note while doing this exercise: 1) When you are raising your foot, relax the hip on that side of the body so that your hips will stay straight. 2) Try to keep the knee of the raised foot out to the side. Now bring your right foot up the side of your left leg again as described above (1, 2, 3, 4); then raise the left heel off the floor — remember to pull in your stomach muscles — as you stay in the same position with the right leg (5, 6, 7, 8, 1, 2, 3, 4); lower left heel to the floor as you bring right leg down as described above (5, 6, 7, 8). Do the entire exercise once again on the right, and then repeat the entire exercise with the right hand on bar, raising the left leg to the same counts.

Slide the toes of your right foot up the side of your left leg.

21

Exercise IX *Body Roll Stretch* This is a good exercise for stretching the arms, spine and upper thighs.

a) Stand facing the bar, at a distance of about 3 feet. Place your arms at your sides and your feet in first position parallel. Raise hands above your head and reach as far as you can toward the ceiling (1, 2, 3, 4). Then reach the tips of the fingers forward toward the bar, bringing your head, shoulders and torso forward with you—remember to pull in your stomach as you go over—until the fingertips touch the bar (5, 6, 7, 8). Your back should be flat, with the torso, shoulders and face parallel to the floor. Now come up to the original position by raising your arms and pulling in your stomach muscles. Let the torso straighten first, then the shoulders, and then the head (1, 2, 3, 4). Finally the arms go back down to the sides (5, 6, 7, 8). Repeat entire exercise.

b) Start in the same position you used in "Body Roll Stretch A." Stretch arms up above your head again (1, 2, 3, 4) and go forward toward the bar with fingers, head, shoulders and torso until you can grab the bar with both hands (5, 6, 7, 8). The back should be flat, and your elbows should be straight. (If they're not, move a little farther away from the bar.)

Imagine that someone has punched you in the stomach so that your stomach contracts while the back becomes slightly rounded (1, 2, 3, 4); release the stomach by pushing the stomach flat again (5, 6, 7, 8); go into contraction again (1, 2, 3, 4); release (5, 6, 7, 8). Now come up by raising your arms and straightening the body by using the stomach muscles (1–8). Repeat the entire exercise.

c) Start with your body facing the bar again and go over toward the bar as you did in the previous stretch exercise (1–8); now with the back flat as before and hands on bar with elbows straight, contract stomach, chest and shoulders (1–8). You should feel as if everything is pulling in so that your back becomes rounded and you can feel the pelvis coming forward and the buttocks straightening up. Now release, starting with the stomach, then the chest and then the shoulders, until the back is flat once more (1–8); come up to the original position by using the stomach muscles (1–8); release (1–8). Repeat entire exercise.

d) With body facing the bar go forward again as in previous exercises (1–8); with both hands on bar and elbows straight, contract the stomach and then the chest, shoulders and neck until your chin is touching the top of the chest (1–8); continue the contraction movement until the body is straight with only the fingertips holding on to the bar (1–8); then go over again toward the bar until the back is flat once more (1–8). Now repeat the body contraction, only this time take four counts to contract (1–4); continue to come up (5–8); go back over to the flat back position (1–8); then contract body (1–4); continue up to straight back (5–8); put your arms at your sides and relax body (1–8). Repeat entire exercise.

Stand facing the bar. (This side view will show you what your body should look like after you've bent over.) Remember to pull in your stomach as you bring your head, shoulders and torso forward until your fingertips touch the bar and your back is flat.

Exercise X *Forward Extensions* Place your left hand on the bar, and hold your right arm out to the side in second position. Your left foot should be straight and flat on the floor, and the ball of your right foot should be on the floor behind the left heel and slightly to the right. Both knees are bent. Straighten your left knee as you point your right toes downward, and then bring your right toes up to your left calf (1, 2); keeping the left knee

Bend both knees while keeping your left foot flat on the floor. The ball of your right foot should be on the floor behind the left heel and slightly to the right.

straight, extend or stretch your right leg in front of your body as you straighten the right knee (3, 4); retrace your movements by bending your right knee as your right toes come back to side of left calf (5, 6); begin to bend left knee as you lower ball of right foot to original starting position (7, 8). (Both knees are now bent.) Repeat this exercise seven times. Now turn your body so that your right hand is on the bar and your left arm is out to the side in second position. Repeat entire exercise eight times.

Keeping your left knee straight, stretch your right leg in front of you as you straighten your right knee.

To finish the Forward Extension, begin to bend your left knee
as you lower your right foot to the starting position.

Begin with your left foot flat on the floor
and slightly turned out and the
ball of your right foot, also slightly turned out,
in back of your left heel.

Exercise XI *Side Extensions* Stand with your left
hand on the bar, and your right arm out to the side in second
position. Your left foot should be flat on the floor and slightly
turned out. The ball of your right foot should be in back of
the left heel, slightly turned out. Both knees are bent.
Straighten your left knee as you point your right toes downward and bring your right toes up to the left calf (1, 2); keeping the left knee straight, extend or stretch the right leg to
the side of your body as you straighten the right knee (3, 4).
As you do this, don't try for height; rather, be sure that the
hips stay forward and on an even plane. Retrace your
movements by bending right knee as right toe comes back to
side of left calf (5, 6); begin to bend left knee as you lower
right foot to original starting position (7, 8). Both knees are
now bent. Repeat this exercise seven times. Then turn to
other side and repeat eight times on left side.

Exercise XII *Double-Time Extensions* These are the same as "Forward Extensions" and "Side Extensions," but they're done twice as fast. Place your left hand on the bar, and hold your right arm out to the side in second position. Your left foot should be straight and flat on the floor, and the ball of your right foot should be on the floor behind the left heel and slightly to the right. Both knees are bent. Straighten your left knee as you point your right toes downward and bring right toe up to left calf (1); extend right leg to the front as you straighten right knee (2); bring right toe back to left calf (3); lower right foot to original position (4). Repeat to front using counts 5 through 8. Repeat six times to front. Then turn to the other side and repeat eight times on the left. Now do the extensions to the side. Extend your right leg to the right side eight times and then turn and repeat extensions to the left side eight times. This is important, as you will be using these extensions in combinations that must be done quickly.

Extend your right leg in front
as you straighten your right knee.

Exercise XIII *Back Kicks* Face the bar with feet in first position turned out, just far enough away so that your hands will touch the bar. Extend right foot forward. Place both hands on the bar. Slide right foot back through first position, continuing into a backward kick (1, 2); bring right foot back through first position to starting position (3, 4). It will help if you think of your foot and leg as a pendulum. Kick right foot back again (5, 6); return to starting position (7, 8). Do back kicks six more times. Then, with the left foot extended forward, repeat entire exercise for a total of eight times.

With both of your hands on the bar, slide your right foot back into a backward kick.

ISOLATIONS

An isolation is the very smooth movement of one part of the body, done while the rest of the body remains still. For instance, you might move your head without moving any other part of your body.

HEAD ISOLATION

BODY PLACEMENT:
The body faces front, with the hips and shoulders straight. The feet are in second position parallel. The weight of the body is forward on the balls of the feet, not leaning back on the heels. Arms hang loosely at your sides.

MUSIC: Slow or Slow Percussion tempo

COUNTS:
A. *Side to Side:* Use two counts for each movement. 1, 2; 3, 4; 5, 6; 7, 8.
B. *Back and Forward:* Use two counts for each movement. 1, 2; 3, 4; 5, 6; 7, 8.
C. *Head Roll:* Use two counts for each movement. 1, 2; 3, 4; 5, 6; 7, 8.

DESCRIPTION OF STEP:
a) Side to Side: Now that you are properly placed, close your eyes and picture your shoulders in your mind—imagine them hanging and dropping down to the floor. (This will relax the shoulders so that you can get the most stretch and suppleness possible from the exercises.)

Pretend that your chin is resting on an imaginary shelf, at its own level, being careful not to push your head forward. On two counts (1, 2), turn head smoothly, first to the right, and focus on some object on the right side of the room that is at eye level; then, remembering the shelf in your mind, turn head back to the starting position or center of your body, which I will hereafter refer to as the center (3, 4); then turn head smoothly to left side, focusing on something at eye level on the left side of the room (5, 6); then rotate head back to center (7, 8). Repeat entire exercise. Then repeat the exercise a bit faster—turn head to right side (1); back to center (2); to the left (3); back to center (4); right (5); center (6); left (7); center (8). Now repeat the exercise to the right and left without stopping at the center. Begin with head at center and turn head to right (1, 2); turn to left (3, 4); turn to right (5, 6); turn to left (7, 8). Then repeat this continuous exercise a bit faster. Turn head to right (1); to left (2); to right (3); to left (4); to right (5); to left (6); to right (7); to left (8). Remember to keep your shoulders relaxed so that you will not hurt your neck.

Side to Side: Turn your head to the right, focusing on some object at eye level *(above)*.

Back and Forward: Drop your head back so that you can see the ceiling *(below)*.

b) Back and Forward: Body should be positioned exactly as it was in the first exercise. Keeping the shoulders relaxed, drop the head back so that you can see the ceiling (1, 2); bring the head back to the center (3, 4); then drop the head forward so that the chin almost touches the chest (5, 6) — don't worry if the chin cannot touch the chest; bring head back to the center (7, 8). Repeat entire exercise — head back (1, 2); center (3, 4); forward (5, 6); center (7, 8). Then repeat the exercise faster: head back (1); center (2); forward (3); center (4); back (5); center (6); forward (7); center (8). Now repeat without stopping in the center: back (1); forward (2); back (3); forward (4); back (5); forward (6); back (7); forward (8).

c) Head Roll: Position the body the same way, remembering to keep the shoulders relaxed. Begin by dropping your head loosely to the right shoulder — as if trying to touch the shoulder with your ear (1, 2); now start to roll the head back very slowly until you feel your neck stretching (3, 4); continue to roll the head to the left side, as if trying to touch the left shoulder with your left ear (5, 6); now continue to roll the head forward so that your chin touches your chest (7, 8). Repeat this entire exercise to the right side and then repeat two times starting to the left side. Then repeat faster to the right by rolling the entire head on four counts. Roll head to right side (1); back (2); left side (3); front (4). Repeat again to right side and then repeat two times to left side.

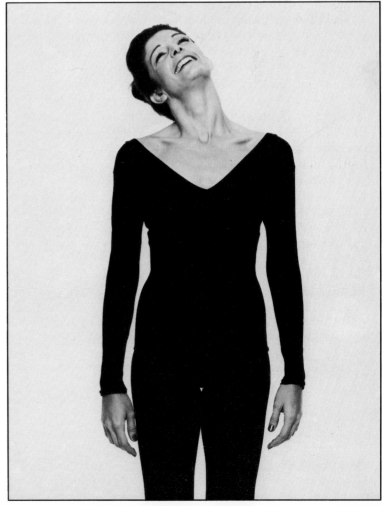

Back and Forward: Drop your head forward so that your chin almost touches your chest *(above)*.

Head Roll: Roll your head back very slowly until you feel your neck stretching *(below)*.

SHOULDER ISOLATION

BODY PLACEMENT:
The body faces front, with the hips and shoulders straight. The feet are in second position parallel. The weight of the body is forward on the balls of the feet, not leaning back on the heels. Arms hang loosely at your sides.

MUSIC: Slow or Slow Percussion tempo

COUNTS:
A. *Raising and Lowering:* Use one count for each movement.
   1, 2, 3, 4, 5, 6, 7, 8.
B. *Shoulder Roll:* Use two counts up and forward and two counts back to starting position.
   1, 2; 3, 4; 5, 6; 7, 8.
C. *Opposite Shoulders:* Use two counts to raise both shoulders, two counts for opposing movement front and back, two counts to raise both shoulders and two counts for reverse opposing movement front and back.
   1, 2; 3, 4; 5, 6; 7, 8.

DESCRIPTION OF STEP:
   a) Raising and Lowering: Raise the right shoulder toward the right ear (1); lower the shoulder to a position referred to as "down," that is, level with the opposite shoulder (2); now repeat the same on the left side— left shoulder up (3); down (4); then repeat on the right (5, 6); and then on the left (7, 8). Repeat this exercise with *both* shoulders. Raise both shoulders (1); lower (2); raise (3); lower (4); raise (5); lower (6); raise (7); lower (8).

Raising and Lowering:
Raise your left shoulder up toward your left ear.

b) Shoulder Roll: Raise right shoulder up and then forward in a semicircle toward the front, as though you were drawing an imaginary horseshoe with the top of the shoulder (1, 2); bring the shoulder up and back in a semicircle to the starting position (3, 4); then repeat with right shoulder up and forward (5, 6); and back to starting position (7, 8). Now do this with left shoulder: forward (1, 2); to starting position (3, 4); forward (5, 6); to starting position (7, 8). Then repeat on right side going to the back: semicircle to the back (1, 2); to starting position (3, 4); back (5, 6); to starting position (7, 8). Now repeat on left side going to the back (1–8). Repeat forward and back with *both* shoulders: both shoulders forward (1, 2); to starting position (3, 4); both shoulders back (5, 6); to starting position (7, 8). Repeat forward and back with both shoulders again (1–8).

c) Opposite Shoulders: This time put your hands on your hips. Raise both shoulders up toward your ears (1, 2); push right shoulder forward as you pull the left shoulder back, still continuing to use the same semicircular, horseshoe motion (3, 4); then raise both shoulders again (5, 6); and reverse, pulling right shoulder back and left shoulder forward (7, 8). Repeat entire exercise three times. Then do the same exercise, but starting forward with left shoulder this time. Raise both shoulders up toward the ears (1, 2); push left shoulder forward as you pull the right shoulder back (3, 4); raise both shoulders again (5, 6); and reverse, pulling left shoulder back and right shoulder forward (7, 8). Repeat this exercise three times.

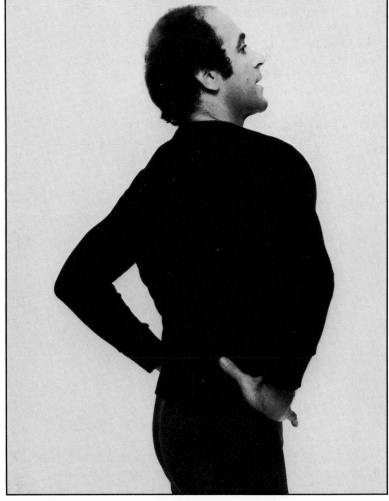

Shoulder Roll: Raise your right shoulder up and then bring it forward in a semicircle toward the front (*above*).

Opposite Shoulders: With both hands on your hips, raise both shoulders up and then push your right shoulder forward as you pull your left shoulder back (*below*).

RIB-CAGE ISOLATION

BODY PLACEMENT:
The body faces front, with the hips and shoulders straight. The feet are in second position parallel. The weight of the body is forward on the balls of the feet, not leaning back on the heels. Hands are placed at the waist.

MUSIC: Slow or Slow Percussion tempo

COUNTS:
A. *Side to Side:* Use two counts to right. Use two counts to center. Use two counts to left and two counts to center.
1, 2; 3, 4; 5, 6; 7, 8.
B. *Forward and Back:* Use two counts forward. Use two counts to center. Use two counts to back and two counts to center.
1, 2; 3, 4; 5, 6; 7, 8.
C. *Circle Rib Cage:* Use two counts to right. Use two counts to back. Use two counts to left and two counts to front.
1, 2; 3, 4; 5, 6; 7, 8.

DESCRIPTION OF STEP:
We will now do an exercise for the rib cage. To find the bottom of the rib cage, place your hands on your waist and raise your index fingers about 1½ inches. There you will find a bone or protrusion which is the bottom of the rib cage.

a) Side to Side: Place your hands at the bottom of the rib cage so that you can see and feel the rib cage move. Imagine that the bottom of the rib cage is pushing some object away to the right. This should cause you to move the rib cage only, but keep your hands at the bottom of the rib cage so that you can feel the movement (1, 2); return the rib cage to the center or starting position (3, 4); now push away some imaginary object with the bottom of the left side of the rib cage (5, 6); return to center (7, 8). Repeat this exercise. Now repeat the exercise on a one-count: rib cage to the right (1); center (2); to left (3); center (4); right (5); center (6); left (7); center (8). Now let's do the rib-cage isolations without stopping in the center, going straight from the right to the left side. Start in the center and go to the right (1); left (2); right (3); left (4); right (5); left (6); right (7); left (8).

Side to Side: Imagine that you are pushing some object away to the right with your rib cage.

b) Forward and Back: Place your hands at the bottom of the rib cage. Imagine that your rib cage is pushing some imaginary object forward (1, 2); bring it back to the center or starting position (3, 4); now pretend that someone has punched you in the space between the two bottom ribs so that your rib cage moves back (5, 6); bring the rib cage back to the center (7, 8). Repeat this exercise. Now repeat it on a one-count: rib cage forward (1); center (2); back (3); center (4); forward (5); center (6); back (7); center (8). We will now do this exercise without stopping in the center: begin at the center and go forward (1); back (2); forward (3); back (4); forward (5); back (6); forward (7); back (8).

c) Circle Rib Cage: Starting from the center position, move your rib cage to the right (1, 2); bring it to the back (3, 4); then to the left side (5, 6); and then bring the rib cage forward (7, 8). Repeat this exercise, beginning to the right side (1–8). Then repeat two times to the left side.

Forward and Back:
Push your rib cage forward.

Move your rib cage back by imagining
that someone has punched you between
your two bottom ribs.

HIP ISOLATION

BODY PLACEMENT:
The body faces front, with the hips and shoulders straight. The feet are in second position parallel. The weight of the body is forward on the balls of the feet, not leaning back on the heels. Hands are placed at the back of each hip. Your hips should be very relaxed so that they may move loosely.

MUSIC: Slow or Percussion tempo

COUNTS:
A. *Side to Side:* Use two counts to right. Use two counts to center. Use two counts to left and two counts to center.
   1, 2; 3, 4; 5, 6; 7, 8.
B. *Forward and Back:* Use two counts forward. Use two counts to center. Use two counts to back and two counts to center.
   1, 2; 3, 4; 5, 6; 7, 8.
C. *Circle Hips:* Use two counts to right. Use two counts to back. Use two counts left and two counts forward.
   1, 2; 3, 4; 5, 6; 7, 8.

Side to Side: Move your right hip to the right side.

DESCRIPTION OF STEP:
a) Side to Side: Move the right hip to the right side so that you can feel the right hand being pushed out by the right hip (1, 2); bring hip back to center or starting position (3, 4); now move the left hip to the left so that you feel the left hand being pushed out (5, 6); bring hip back to the center (7, 8). Repeat this exercise, only this time start on the left side (1–8). Now repeat on a one-count: hip to right (1); center (2); left (3); center (4); right (5); center (6); left (7); center (8). Do this again, starting to the left. Now repeat without stopping in the center: right (1); left (2); right (3); left (4); right (5); left (6); right (7); left (8). Repeat this exercise again, starting to the left (1–8).

Now move your left hip to the left side.

b) Forward and Back: We will now go forward and back with the hips. Push the pelvis forward and up (1, 2); return hips to center (3, 4); push the hips back so that the buttocks stick out (5, 6); back to center (7, 8). Rotate the hips under and back in a smooth motion. Repeat this exercise, going to the back first (1–8). Now repeat on a one-count: forward (1); center (2); back (3); center (4); forward (5); center (6); back (7); center (8). Now repeat without stopping in the center: forward (1); back (2); forward (3); back (4); forward (5); back (6); forward (7); back (8).

c) Circle Hips: Push right hip to right side (1, 2); hips to back (3, 4); left hip to left side (5, 6); hips and pelvis forward (7, 8). Repeat, starting to the right side (1–8). Now do the same thing, starting to the left side: left hip to left side (1, 2); hips to back (3, 4); right hip to right side (5, 6); pelvis and hips forward (7, 8). Repeat exercise starting to left side.

Forward and Back: Push your pelvis forward and up.

Push your hips back so that your buttocks stick out.

KNEE ISOLATION

BODY PLACEMENT:
Begin with the body facing front and the feet placed in second position turned out. Arms hang loosely at your sides.

MUSIC: Slow or Percussion tempo

COUNTS:
Use one count to push right heel off the floor. Use one count to lower right heel.
1, 2. Repeat: 3, 4; 5, 6; 7, 8. Reverse: 1, 2; 3, 4; 5, 6; 7, 8.

DESCRIPTION OF STEP:
This exercise will stretch and strengthen the calf muscles. (You should realize that using muscles does not make that part of the body larger or "fatter.") With the weight on the left foot, lift the right heel off the floor leaving the ball of the right foot on the floor (1). The toes should be spread out to give better balance and to prevent cramping. Lower the right heel down to the floor (2); raise it up again in the same way (3); lower it (4). Continue doing this until the count of 8. Now place the weight on the right foot and lift the left heel off the floor leaving the ball of the left foot on the floor (1); lower the left heel down to the floor (2); raise it again the same way (3); lower it (4). Continue doing this until the count of eight.

KNEE SEMICIRCLE

BODY PLACEMENT:
Begin with the body facing front and the feet placed in second position turned out. Arms hang loosely at your sides.

MUSIC: Medium tempo with a strong beat

COUNTS:
Use two counts to raise right heel. Use two counts to make a semicircle toward the left knee. Use two counts to retrace the semicircle back to starting position. Use two counts to lower right heel.
1, 2; 3, 4; 5, 6; 7, 8. Reverse: 1, 2; 3, 4; 5, 6; 7, 8.

DESCRIPTION OF STEP:
Place all your weight on the left foot so that you get the feeling that your left foot is "glued" to the floor. Raise the heel of the right foot (1, 2); turn the right side of your body toward the left, making a semicircle with the right knee toward the left (3, 4); retrace the semicircle back to the starting position with the knee, moving your body back to its original position (5, 6); lower the right heel (7, 8). Repeat the same exercise starting with the left foot. Keep your weight firmly on the right foot and raise the heel of your left foot (1, 2); turn the left side of your body toward the right, making a semicircle with the left knee toward the right (3, 4); retrace the semicircle back to the starting position with the knee, moving your body back as well (5, 6); lower the left heel (7, 8). Now repeat this entire exercise beginning with raising the left heel, and then repeat the entire exercise beginning with raising the right heel. Remember that the leg of the foot that is "glued" to the ground shouldn't move at all. You should be using your stomach muscles to twist the body so that you don't put any strain on the back and knees.

DANCERNASTICS

We will start our floor work by stretching. Do each stretch until you feel that you can do it smoothly and without strain, almost like a dance movement, rather than a calisthenic exercise. A good album to use for these exercises is *Saturday Night Fever*. Since it is a long-playing record, you won't have to worry about changing the album during the exercises, which would disturb your concentration.

REACHING FOR LIFE

If you can recall a morning when you woke up feeling absolutely wonderful and you then stretched your arms up to the ceiling, you will understand this exercise. This stretch is good for the back and the arms and for releasing tension. Stand with your feet in second position parallel. Your arms are above your head and your shoulders should be down. Reach your right arm up to the ceiling as though you are reaching for a rope that is hanging down just beyond your reach (1, 2, 3, 4); then reach the left arm the same way (5, 6, 7, 8). Keep doing this exercise until your body feels stretched, stronger and warmed up.

TORSO STRETCH

A good exercise for reducing the waist, stretching the torso, the back of the thighs and the inner thighs, and strengthening the abdominal muscles. Stand with the feet in second position parallel, about one foot apart, arms hanging at your sides. Reach over to the right side with the right arm, shoulder and head (1, 2, 3, 4); come up by using the stomach muscles (5, 6, 7, 8). When doing the reach over, you should feel that the whole upper torso is falling over to the side. Be sure that the hips and shoulders stay facing front. Coming up, imagine the stomach pushing into the spine, and the spine pushing into the stomach. Now go over to the left side (1, 2, 3, 4); come up (5, 6, 7, 8). Continue doing this exercise, first to the right side and then to the left, several more times, always using four counts to go over and four counts to come up.

BODY CIRCLE

A stretch for the upper hips, thighs and arms. Place your feet about a foot apart in second position parallel. Clasp your hands over your head with the palms turned up. Turn upper torso to the right side (1, 2); reach torso and arms forward and down to right toe (3); continue reaching, and bend both knees to take the strain and pressure off the back (4); circle the body to the center and then to the left side (5); straighten both knees (6); bring body up to original position (7, 8). Then begin again to the left side. Turn upper torso to left side (1, 2); reach torso and arms forward and down to left toe (3); continue reaching to left toe, and bend both knees (4); circle the body to the center and then to the right side (5); straighten both knees (6); bring body up to original position (7, 8). Do this several more times.

LEG EXTENSION

A good stretch for the abdominal muscles and the pelvis area. Lie on the floor with your arms stretched out to your sides, palms turned up, feet together and knees up. Make sure that the small of your back is pressed down into the floor so that there is very little or no space between the floor and the back of your waist. Begin by thinking of the stomach muscles pressing into the spine. Raise the right foot so that it is next to the calf of the left leg (1, 2); continue to raise the foot and extend the leg until the knee of the right leg is straight and the toes of the right foot are pointed (3, 4); bring right foot back opposite left calf (5, 6); lower right foot back to starting position (7, 8). Now repeat with the left foot. Raise the left foot so that it is next to the calf of the right leg (1, 2); continue to raise the foot and extend the leg until the knee of the left leg is straight and the toes of the left foot are pointed (3, 4); bring left foot back opposite right calf (5, 6); lower left foot back to starting position (7, 8). Again, repeat this on both legs until you feel stretched.

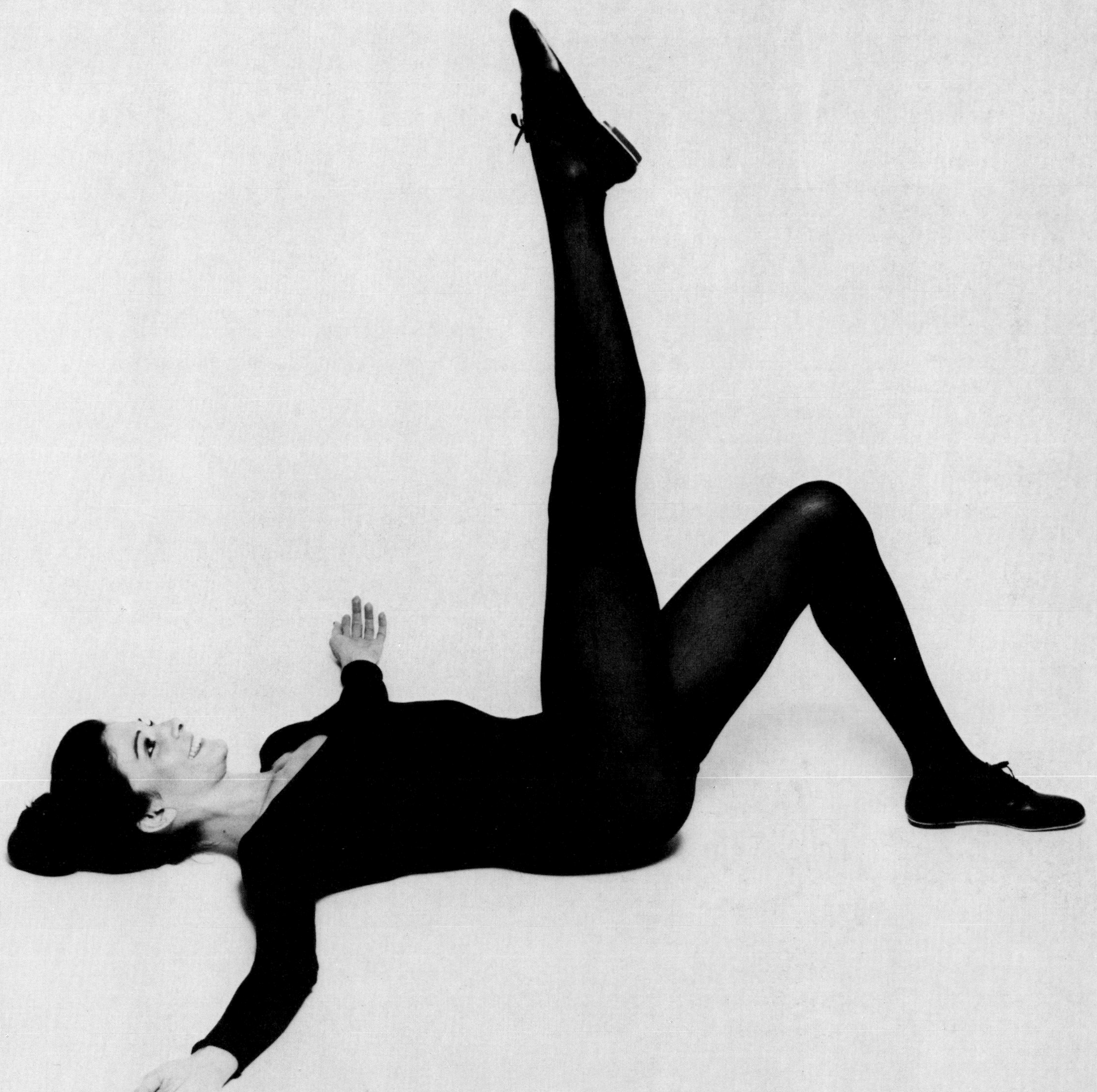

PELVIC LIFT

Good for upper thighs, waist and stomach, and for strengthening the back muscles. Lie on the floor. Knees are bent, with back flat on the floor and arms down to the sides with the palms facing up. Keep the feet flat on the floor during this entire exercise. Now pretend that attached to both pelvic bones there are two ropes from the ceiling that are pulling you upward. This should bring your pelvis, stomach and lower back up off the floor while your feet and hands stay on the floor. Push up as was just described (1, 2, 3, 4); hold this position and really feel the stretching of those parts of the body that are off the floor (5, 6, 7, 8). Be sure to keep breathing and to relax the neck and back. Then return to your starting position (1–8), making sure to take the full eight counts coming down. This will not only give you a fuller stretch, but it will also guarantee that you won't injure your lower back by coming down too fast. Repeat this once again. You can add one additional stretch each time you do this exercise.

THE ROW BOAT

Strengthens and tightens the abdominal muscles. Begin by lying flat on the floor with arms at your sides, palms down. Now bring up your knees and upper torso simultaneously while moving your arms out straight in front of you (1, 2, 3, 4). You should imagine that you are rowing a boat: grab on to imaginary oars as you come up and as you go back down (5, 6, 7, 8). Come up (1, 2, 3, 4); lower the body back to the original position (5, 6, 7, 8). Repeat this three or four times at first, but try to increase the amount with each practice period.

PANCAKE STRETCH

For stretching the spine, the back of the legs and the stomach. Begin sitting up with your back perfectly straight, your legs stretched out in front with the toes pointed, and your arms up above your head. Now stretch your arms above your head as though you are trying to grab two ropes that are hanging directly above you just out of your reach. When you've reached as high as you can, then try to reach your fingertips to your toes (1, 2, 3, 4). (You will not be able to touch your toes until you are more stretched out by practice, so just go over as far as you can without hurting yourself. The "pancake" effect of being fully stretched out so that your body is flat over on your legs will come later.) Now grab the back of your calves with your hands (you can reach down to your ankles if you are stretched enough) and hold while you continue to stretch (5, 6, 7, 8,); now release the hands and push them forward and up as you come back to the original position (1–8). Be sure to use the stomach muscles to come back up so that there is no strain on the back. Repeat this exercise three or four more times, and do it more frequently as you become more stretched out.

Start by stretching your arms above your head as high as you can.

Begin to stretch over.

Don't worry if you can't reach your ankles—just stretch as far as is comfortable.

OVER WE GO

This exercise is for the waistline, hips and back. Sit on the floor with your back straight. Spread your legs apart as far as you can in front of you and point your toes, trying to keep the knees straight, even though you may not be able to stretch the legs out very far. As you do these stretches the legs will become more limber, and eventually you will be able to stretch them out a good deal further. Now extend your arms over your head with your hands clasped and palms facing the ceiling. Turn the upper torso and arms toward the right leg and reach both the arms and the torso over toward the right foot (1, 2, 3, 4). Do this by pulling in the stomach muscles while pretending that your hands are pushing something away that is at

Clasp your hands over your head while spreading your legs apart. Be sure that your knees are straight, and don't worry if your legs are not very far apart at the beginning.

the end of the toes on your right foot. Do not force your body to bend forward any more than you are able. The only thing that forcing can accomplish is to make you so sore that you won't want to do the exercise again. Now come back up to the starting position, using the stomach muscles once again (5, 6, 7, 8). Then turn the upper torso and arms to the front and reach forward as though you were pushing something away in front of you (1, 2, 3, 4); come back up to the starting position, using the stomach muscles (5, 6, 7, 8). Turn the upper torso toward the left leg, and this time stretch over to the left foot (1, 2, 3, 4); come back up to the starting position (5, 6, 7, 8). Now repeat to the right side, center and left side. This will be enough for the first day; increase the number with practice.

Using your stomach muscles, reach your arms and torso over toward the right foot. Again, be careful not to force your body forward any more than is comfortable.

LEG CIRCLES

For stomach and thighs. Lie flat on your back with your arms stretched out to the sides, palms turned up, and your legs in front of you with your toes pointed. Bend your left knee while keeping your left foot on the floor. The right leg should remain straight with the toes pointed. Now you are going to make circles with the right leg by raising it up toward the ceiling (1); moving the leg to the side (2); down toward the floor, without touching the floor (3); then back to the starting position (4). Make three more circles without stopping in-between. Then reverse the circle by moving your right leg inward or counterclockwise. To make the inward circle, start with your leg pointed up in the air again; lower the leg until it almost touches the floor (1); then bring it out to the side (2); then over (3); and up until you reach the starting position once again (4). Be sure the circles are continuous. Do this four times. Now repeat the same thing with the left leg. Start by bending the knee of the right leg so that the right foot remains on the floor. The left leg should be straight with toes pointed. Now raise left leg off the floor up toward the ceiling and circle the left leg outward to four counts. Do this three more times. Now reverse the left leg circle so that you will be making an inward circle. Do this four times, making sure you take only four counts for each circle. This exercise may be difficult at the beginning because it really demands strong stomach muscles, but as you do it more and more, you will discover your stomach becoming flat, hard and strong.

With your left knee bent, point the toes of your right foot toward the ceiling.

Move your right leg to the side.

As you move your right foot down toward the floor,
be careful that your foot doesn't actually touch the floor.

UP, UP AND AWAY

For waist, stomach and back. Sit on the floor with your body facing forward and your legs out in front of you. Now switch the weight of your body to the left hip and bend the right knee, keeping the right foot on the floor. The right arm should rest across the right knee, and the left hand should be flat on the floor in back of your left hip so that the torso is turned to the left. Pull in your stomach muscles and put your weight on the palm of your left hand so that you can push the hips off the floor and thrust the pelvis toward the ceiling. As you do this, lift your right arm and your face toward the ceiling. This action should raise the left thigh and calf off the floor, while leaving the outside of the left foot and the ball of the right foot on the floor. Take four counts to go up, hold for four counts and lower to eight counts, being sure to use your stomach muscles. Repeat on the left side.

Now turn to the right, putting the weight on the right hip. Bend the left knee, keeping the left foot on the floor. The left arm should rest across the left knee, and the right hand should be flat on the floor in back of the right hip so that the torso is turned to the right. Pull in your stomach muscles and put your weight on the palm of your right hand so that you can push the hips off the floor and thrust the pelvis toward the ceiling. As you do this, lift your left arm and your face toward the ceiling. This action should raise the right thigh and calf off the floor, while leaving the outside of the right foot and the ball of your left foot on the floor. Take four counts to go up, hold for four counts and lower to eight counts. Repeat on the right side.

LEG LIFTS

These exercises will firm, strengthen and reduce the thighs if you do them exactly as described.

a) Begin by lying flat on your back with the legs stretched out in front of you. Place your arms at your sides, palms up. Making sure the upper torso stays on the floor, point the toes and lift the right leg just 4 or 5 inches off the floor (1, 2, 3, 4); keep the leg there and stretch it by pointing the toes even harder and stretching the shin muscles in the upper calf (5, 6, 7, 8); lower the right leg very slowly (1, 2, 3, 4, 5, 6, 7, 8) by using the stomach muscles. Lift left leg (1, 2, 3, 4); stay and stretch (5, 6, 7, 8); lower leg very slowly (1, 2, 3, 4, 5, 6, 7, 8). Repeat this as many times as you can without getting tired.

b) Roll over to your left side and prop up your head with your left hand. The palm of your right hand is on the floor in front of your chest so that the right elbow is bent. Point your toes. Now lift the right leg only 4 or 5 inches off the floor (1, 2, 3, 4); stay there and stretch the leg (5, 6, 7, 8); lower the leg back down to the floor (1, 2, 3, 4, 5, 6, 7, 8). As you do this exercise try to keep the body in a straight line. Again, be sure to use the stomach muscles both to raise and lower the leg. Repeat this exercise with the right leg about six or seven times, and increase the amount with each practice period. Roll over to the right side, and repeat this exercise with the left leg seven or eight times.

c) Roll over on your stomach and place your hands, one on top of the other, underneath your head so that your cheek is resting on the back of one hand. Point your toes. Keeping your back straight, and using the stomach muscles, raise the right leg only 3 or 4 inches off the floor (1, 2, 3, 4); hold and stretch the leg (5, 6, 7, 8); lower the right leg to the floor (1, 2, 3, 4, 5, 6, 7, 8). In this position you will feel the stomach muscles working even harder. Then repeat this with the left leg. Raise the left leg only 3 or 4 inches off the floor (1, 2, 3, 4); hold and stretch the leg (5, 6, 7, 8); lower the left leg to the floor (1, 2, 3, 4, 5, 6, 7, 8). Continue to do this with the right and left leg, making sure that you don't get overtired.

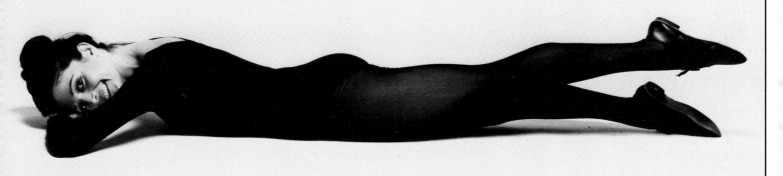

ROCKING HORSE

This exercise stretches the stomach, back and legs, as well as the arms and neck. Lie on your stomach and lift up your head so that you are looking at the ceiling. Bend your knees and grab your ankles if you are stretched enough, or your calves if you are not. Your back should be rounded, with just your stomach and the tops of your thighs touching the floor. Rock your body forward and back as many times as you can without discomfort. Don't worry about counts — just do it to your own rhythm. Some people may find it easier to do it fast. This is a lot of fun when you are stretched out, and when you let your body take over the movement.

CENTER FLOOR WORK

Now you are going to start doing some basic dance movements. In order to achieve the balance and strength needed for the following lessons these exercises are done without support. If you keep firmly in your mind the image of the stomach and spine being pulled in together, you may find it easier to keep your balance. You also may want to stand in front of a mirror.

BODY SWAY

BODY PLACEMENT:
Stand with the body facing front. Place the feet apart, in second position turned out. Arms and fingers are outstretched at shoulder level.

MUSIC: Slow and Dreamy tempo

COUNTS:
Use eight counts to "lunge" the right knee. Use eight counts to straighten and return to starting position.
1–8; 1–8. Reverse: 1–8; 1–8.

DESCRIPTION OF STEP:
Keeping the left leg and knee straight, bend the right knee outward over the right toes, keeping the right foot on the floor and "lunge," by pressing the right knee toward the floor in that position (1, 2). Press three more times (3–4, 5–6, 7–8). (Be sure to keep the hips and body straight forward while you do this exercise.) Then make sure the stomach muscles are pulled in and slowly straighten the right knee to eight counts until both knees are in their original position (1–8). Repeat this entire exercise, beginning with the left knee bending and stretching (1–8) and coming back to starting position (1–8). Repeat exercise to both the right and left, trying to stretch even further. Remember, however, that you should never stretch to the point of pain. You must get more limber gradually, trying to do a little more each time.

TORSO TURN

BODY PLACEMENT:
Stand with the body facing front. Place the feet in second position, turned out. Arms are straight out to your sides in second position, with the palms facing the floor.

MUSIC: Slow and Dreamy tempo

COUNTS:
Use two counts to raise right heel off floor. Use two counts to turn the body toward the left. Use two counts to make a semicircle with the right knee. Use two counts to complete the movement. 1, 2; 3, 4; 5, 6; 7, 8. Retrace: 1, 2; 3, 4; 5, 6; 7, 8.

DESCRIPTION OF STEP:
Start to lower your head toward the right shoulder while stretching your rib cage to the right (1, 2); continue this movement while raising your right heel off the floor (3, 4); keeping your left foot glued to the floor, begin making a semicircle to the left with your right knee while moving the right side of the body to the left. At the same time, raise your right hand, palm up, and begin moving it with the rest of your body (5, 6); complete the movement of the knee to the side, continuing to move your hand across until you can easily look into the right palm. Your left arm will naturally move to a position in back of you—keep the left palm facing down (7, 8). Start to retrace slowly through each movement back to the starting position, being sure that your right heel is the

Lower your head toward your right shoulder while stretching your rib cage to the right.

last thing to return to starting position (1–8). The body should now be facing front, with the arms in second position and the feet in second position turned out. Repeat this exercise beginning to the left. Start to lower your head toward the left shoulder while stretching your rib cage to the left (1, 2); continue this movement while raising your left heel off the floor (3, 4); keeping your right foot glued to the floor, begin making a semicircle to the right with your left knee while moving the left side of the body to the right. At the same time, raise your left hand, palm up, and begin moving it with the rest of your body (5, 6); complete the movement of the knee to the side and raise your left hand enough so that you are looking into the left palm. Your right arm will naturally move to a position in back of you—keep the right palm facing down (7, 8). Start to retrace slowly through each movement back to starting position (1–8).

This is the position you should be in when you finish the step.

FOLD AND UNFOLD

This exercise stretches the back, arms and thighs. Once again, and especially here, you must use the stomach muscles so as not to hurt your back. If you feel any pain in the back itself, stop the exercise and begin again, remembering to pull in the stomach muscles enough.

BODY PLACEMENT:
Stand with the body facing front, arms at your sides. The feet should be slightly apart, toes parallel.

MUSIC: Slow and Dreamy tempo

COUNTS:
Use four counts to stretch your torso. Use four counts to reach for toes. Use eight counts to stretch. Use four counts to bend the knees. Use four counts to return to starting position.
1, 2, 3, 4; 5, 6, 7, 8. 1–8; 1–4; 5–8.
Reverse: 1, 2, 3, 4; 5, 6, 7, 8. 1–8; 1–4; 5–8.

DESCRIPTION OF STEP:
Stretch your arms up over your head, as though you were reaching for something above you. You should now feel a pull in your torso. Take four counts to do this (1, 2, 3, 4). Now start reaching the arms toward the front of the body, and at the same time push the buttocks and the upper thighs back — continue this movement and try to touch the toes (5, 6, 7, 8). Remember to keep the knees straight, even though you may not be able to reach your toes — you will not get a good stretch if you bend your knees. Don't bend over any further than you are able, especially the first time. Now grab on to the back of your knees with your hands. With the elbows bent, try to pull your head into your legs (1–8) — you will really feel the stretch in the thighs here. Now bend the knees and release your hands (1, 2, 3, 4). Slowly, using the stomach muscles, come back up until your arms are at waist level (5, 6, 7, 8); slowly continue to straighten the body and arms until you are in the starting position, with arms over your head (1–8). Repeat this stretch three more times. Do everything very slowly and smoothly.

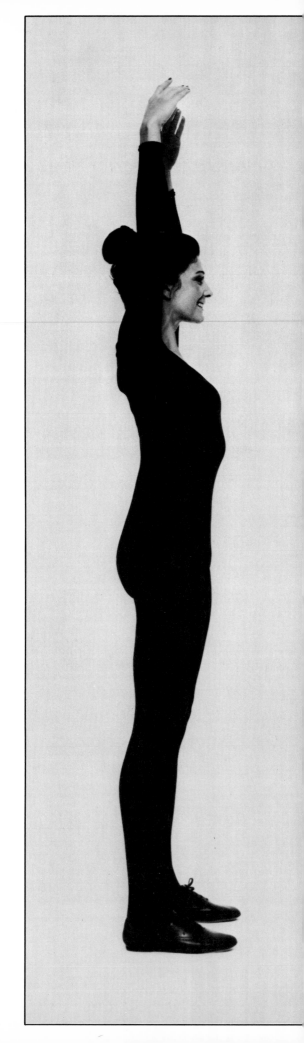

Start in this position, stretching as far as you can so that you feel a pull in your torso.

After you've reached toward your toes,
grab the back of your knees,
bend your elbows and try to pull
your head into your legs.

Bend your knees, release your hands and,
using your stomach muscles,
slowly return to the starting position.

CONTRACTIONS

Contractions are as essential to jazz dancing as are isolations. This exercise begins with a drawing in of the abdominal muscles that causes the thrusting forward of the pelvis, the bending of both knees and the rounding of the back, and then of the shoulders, neck and head in a smooth continuous flow.

BODY PLACEMENT:

Begin with the body facing front and the feet in second position parallel. Place both hands 2 inches in front of the stomach, with palms facing in and fingers outstretched. Arms should form a diamond shape with elbows pointed out.

MUSIC: Bounce tempo with a strong beat

COUNTS:

Use two counts to contract through the center. Use two counts to bend both knees. Use four counts for shoulders, neck and head. Use eight counts to release contraction and return to starting position.
1, 2; 3, 4; 5, 6, 7, 8. 1–8. Reverse: 1, 2; 3, 4; 5, 6, 7, 8. 1–8.

DESCRIPTION OF EXERCISE:

Pretend that someone has punched you in the stomach with a very slow motion. As you imagine this, begin contracting the center of your body (1, 2); continue this movement while bending the knees (3, 4); keep contracting until your back moves forward with the shoulders, neck and head following (5, 6, 7, 8). (The elbows will naturally move forward as you go into the contraction.) Keeping the arms where they are, begin to straighten the body by first pushing the pelvis forward so that the torso, chest, shoulders, neck and head will follow. Take a lot of time coming up—eight counts—so that you can visualize each section of your body straightening. Repeat this exercise. Then do the exercise in half the time—take four counts to go into the contraction and four counts to release it. Repeat this faster contraction one more time.

CONTRACT= SWING THROUGH

BODY PLACEMENT:
Begin with the body facing front. Place the feet slightly apart, toes parallel. Arms are above the head, elbows straight, with the palms facing back. Be sure to keep your shoulders down and your neck relaxed.

MUSIC: Bounce tempo with a strong beat

COUNTS:
Use two counts to contract through the center. Use two counts to bend the knees. Use two counts to continue contraction. Use two counts to swing arms in back.
1, 2; 3, 4; 5, 6; 7, 8.
Begin to retrace this movement. Use two counts to bend the knees. Use two counts to swing arms forward. Use two counts to contract and to start to straighten and two counts to return to starting position.
1, 2; 3, 4; 5, 6; 7, 8.

DESCRIPTION OF STEP:
Again, imagine someone punching you in the stomach. As you do, begin your contraction through the center of your body. At the same time, the elbows start to bend in (1, 2). Continue this movement, which will make the knees bend (3, 4); keep contracting so that the back will continue to move forward with the shoulders, neck and head following (5, 6). As you get to the end of the contraction, your arms should drop down to the sides. Swing your arms out in back of you, while straightening the back and legs (7, 8). Retrace this movement. As you pull the stomach muscles in, bend the knees (1, 2); swing the arms forward (3, 4); begin to straighten the legs slowly (5, 6); continue swinging your arms up slowly while straightening your body until you've returned to the starting position (7, 8). Repeat this exercise, taking eight counts to go into the contraction and eight counts to retrace. Now do the exercise faster, taking four counts to go into the contraction and four counts to retrace: pull stomach in and bend knees (1); move forward with back, neck and head (2); swing arms back (3); straighten knees (4); then retrace. Bend knees and pull stomach muscles in (5); swing arms forward (6); arms continue upward while you begin to straighten the legs (7); body returns to original position (8). Repeat again, four counts to contract and four counts to release.

Imagine that someone has punched you in the stomach as you begin to contract the center of your body. Notice that your elbows will naturally start to bend in.

Continue this movement, bending the knees.

As you finish the contraction, your back, shoulders, neck and head will have moved forward. Your arms drop to the sides.

Swing your arms out in back of you, while straightening your back and legs.

As you begin to retrace the movement, pull your stomach muscles in, bend your knees and swing your arms forward.

JAZZ PLIÉ AND FAR=OUT REACH

BODY PLACEMENT
Begin with the body facing front. Place feet slightly apart but parallel. Arms at sides.

MUSIC: Slow and Dreamy tempo

COUNTS:
Use two counts to step right foot to side. Use two counts to raise left foot off floor. Use two counts to place ball of left foot to side of right heel. Use two counts to raise arms overhead.
1, 2; 3, 4; 5, 6; 7, 8.

Use eight counts to reach arms upward and over and return body to starting position.
1–8.

DESCRIPTION OF STEP:
Step right foot to second position parallel (1, 2); raise left foot about 4 inches off the floor, pointing the toes downward and keeping the left knee facing forward while raising both arms to your sides at shoulder level, palms facing down (3, 4); place ball of left foot to right side of right heel and bend both knees (5, 6); raise both arms overhead, keeping the shoulders down (7, 8). Start to straighten knees and bring the arms down a little (1, 2); reach arms upward and over—left arm toward left front

Raise your left foot off the floor, pointing your toes downward, as you raise your arms.

and right arm toward right back so that the left shoulder will naturally move forward and the right shoulder will naturally move back (3, 4); begin to push downward with palms facing the floor. The head is tilted over the left shoulder and the eyes focused on the left fingertips (5, 6). The knees continue to bend and the arms return to the sides (7, 8). Reverse: Step left foot to second position parallel (1, 2); raise right foot about 4 inches off the floor, pointing the toes downward and keeping the right knee facing forward while raising both arms to your sides at shoulder level, palms facing down (3, 4); place ball of right foot to left side of left heel and bend both knees (5, 6); raise both arms overhead,

keeping the shoulders down (7, 8). Start to straighten knees and bring the arms down a little (1, 2); reach arms upward and over—right arm toward right front and left arm toward left back so that the right shoulder will naturally move forward and the left shoulder will naturally move back (3, 4); begin to push downward with palms facing the floor. The head is tilted over the right shoulder and the eyes focused on the right fingertips (5, 6). The knees continue to bend and arms return to the sides (7, 8).

Place the ball of your left foot to the right side of your right heel and bend both your knees.

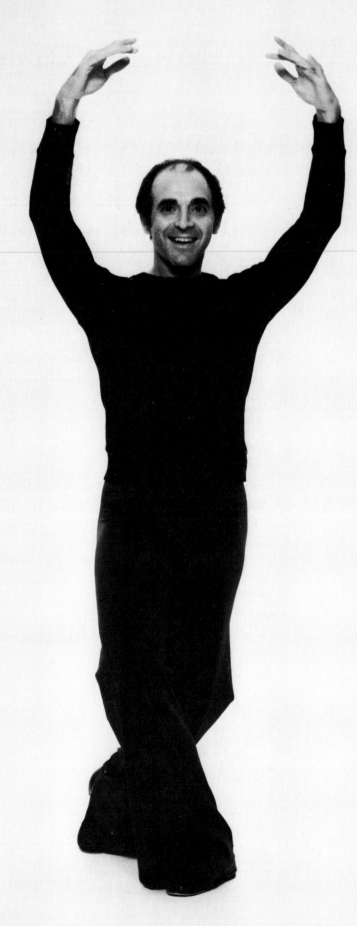

Raise both arms overhead, remembering to keep your shoulders down.

After you've begun to straighten your knees and bring your arms down a little, reach your left arm toward the left front and your right arm toward the right back.

JAZZ WALKS

A jazz walk should be an expression of your individual style. Try to relax while moving freely. And don't let the size of your room constrain you—walk in a circle if the dance space is too small.

WALKING HAPPY

BODY PLACEMENT:
Begin with your weight on the left foot, which should be slightly turned out. Place the toes of the right foot in back of the left heel. The right heel is off the floor. The arms hang loosely at the sides of the body.

MUSIC: Bounce tempo

COUNTS:
A. Walk on each count: 1, 2, 3, 4, 5, 6, 7, 8.
B. Use two counts for each step: 1, 2; 3, 4; 5, 6; 7, 8.

DESCRIPTION OF STEP:
A. Begin by walking across or around the room as though you were walking down the street. Use one count for each step—right foot (1); left foot (2); right (3); left (4); right (5); left (6); right (7); left (8). Walk as much as you want, making sure that you count from one to eight beginning on right foot. Apply the natural arm swing in opposition to the feet (right arm should go forward as the left leg goes forward). If you notice your normal walk in the street, you will see that the arms naturally move in opposition to the feet. That is what we want here.

B. Now we will do the same walk as above, only we will slow it down. This time the toes should be slightly turned out. Step forward about one foot by lifting your right foot about 2 inches off the ground and pointing your toes—as your right foot touches the ground your left arm should swing forward and your right arm should hang by your side (1, 2); now do the same with the left foot, remembering to swing your right arm forward (3, 4); repeat again on the right (5, 6); then on the left (7, 8). Always remember to swing forward the arm that is opposite the moving foot. Continue to do this until the walk becomes effortless. Then repeat the walk, starting with the left foot.

THE SNAPPER

BODY PLACEMENT:
Begin with your weight on the left foot, which should be slightly turned out. Place the toes of the right foot in back of the left heel. The right heel is off the floor. The arms hang loosely at the sides of the body.

MUSIC: Bounce tempo

COUNTS:
Use one count to step and one count to snap. 1, 2, 3, 4, 5, 6, 7, 8.

DESCRIPTION OF STEP:
Step forward with the right foot (1); snap fingers of right hand (2); step forward with the left foot (3); snap fingers of left hand (4); right foot forward (5); right fingers snap (6); left foot forward (7); left fingers snap (8). Continue to do this until it is comfortable for you. Repeat, beginning with the left foot.

CLAP HANDS

BODY PLACEMENT:
Begin with your weight on the left foot, which should be slightly turned out. Place the toes of the right foot in back of the left heel. The right heel is off the floor. The arms hang loosely at the sides of the body.

MUSIC: Bounce tempo

COUNTS:
Use one count to step and one count to clap.
1, 2, 3, 4, 5, 6, 7, 8.

DESCRIPTION OF STEP:
Step forward with the right foot—your upper torso should automatically turn toward the right (1); clap hands in front of chest (2); step forward with the left foot (3); clap hands in front of chest (4); right foot forward (5); clap hands (6); left leg forward (7); clap hands (8). Continue to do this until it feels comfortable, and then repeat it beginning on the left foot. Try to get the feeling of the music as you move.

THE WALKING CHA=CHA

BODY PLACEMENT:
Begin with your weight on the left foot, which should be slightly turned out. Place the toes of the right foot in back of the left heel. The right heel is off the floor. The arms hang loosely at the sides of the body.

MUSIC: Bounce tempo

COUNTS:
Use one count to step right. Pause one count. Use one count to step left. Pause one count. Use one count to step right. Use one count to step left. Use one count to step right. Pause one count.
1, pause 2, 3, pause 4, 5, 6, 7, pause 8.

DESCRIPTION OF STEP:
Step forward on right foot (1); pause (2); step forward on left foot (3); pause (4); then step right foot forward (5); left foot forward (6); right foot forward (7); pause (8). (While you pause, keep your weight on the right foot.) Now repeat, starting with stepping left foot forward (1); pause (2); step right foot forward (3); pause (4); left (5); right (6); left (7); pause (8). (This time, keep your weight on the left foot.) Now you can repeat again, and this time you can either snap your fingers or clap your hands on the pause: right foot forward (1); snap fingers or clap hands, keeping weight on right foot (2); left foot forward (3); snap fingers or clap hands (4); right (5); left (6); right (7); snap or clap (8). Repeat again, starting with left foot: left foot (1); snap or clap (2); right foot (3); snap or clap (4); left (5); right (6); left (7); snap or clap (8). You should now have a good feeling of music and movement.

THE STRUT

BODY PLACEMENT

Begin with your weight on the left foot, which should be slightly turned out. Place the toes of the right foot in back of the left heel. The right heel is off the floor. Place both hands 2 inches in front of the stomach, with palms facing in and fingers outstretched. Arms should form a diamond shape with elbows pointed out.

MUSIC: Bounce tempo

COUNTS:

Use one count to step right. Use one count to touch left. Use one count to step left. Use one count to touch right.
1, 2, 3, 4. Repeat: 5, 6, 7, 8.

DESCRIPTION OF STEP:

Step forward with your right foot, keeping your right toes slightly turned out (1); raise left foot off floor and touch ball of left foot to the left without shifting your weight—as your foot touches the floor, open your arms palms out and move your hands to the sides as though you were pushing something away (2); raise ball of left foot off the floor and place the whole foot in front of the right foot while bringing your hands back to their original diamond position (3); raise right foot off the floor and touch the ball of the right foot to the right side while pushing the hands to the sides again, ending with the palms facing down (4); right foot forward and arms back to original position (5); lift left foot off the floor and touch ball of left foot to left side, while pushing hands away to the sides (6); move left foot forward and bring hands back (7); touch ball of right foot to right side and push hands away (8). Now repeat entire exercise, beginning with the weight on the right foot so that you can start by stepping forward on the left foot: left foot forward with hands in front of you (1); touch ball of right foot to the right while pushing hands away to the sides (2); step forward on right foot, bringing hands back to original position (3); touch the floor with the ball of the left foot and push hands away to the sides (4); move left foot forward and bring hands back to original position (5); touch ball of right foot to right side and push hands away (6); move right foot forward and bring hands back to original position (7); touch ball of left foot to left side and push hands away (8). Keep repeating this exercise, first starting with the right foot and then with the left, until you get the feeling of the step and it becomes comfortable for you. This step is important because it is the basis of the *next step* we are going to do.

Step forward with your right foot.

Touch the ball of your left foot to the left side and move
your hands to the sides as if you were pushing something away.

THE STRUT MOVES

BODY PLACEMENT:
Begin with your weight on the left foot, which should be slightly turned out. Place the toes of the right foot in back of the left heel. The right heel is off the floor. Place both hands two inches in front of the stomach, with palms facing in and fingers outstretched. Arms form a diamond shape with elbows pointed.

MUSIC: Bounce tempo

COUNTS:
This is the first time you will be using the "and" count, or (&), which is explained under the heading of musical terms at the beginning of the book. Use one count to step right. Use the (&) count to step left. Use one count to step right. Use one count to step left. Use the (&) count to step right and one count to step left. 1 & 2, 3 & 4. Repeat: 5 & 6, 7 & 8.

DESCRIPTION OF STEP:
Step forward with your right foot, keeping your toes slightly turned out (1); step left on the ball of your left foot, while pushing your hands away to the side in second position, shifting the weight to the left and bending the left knee (&); step about one foot to the right side with your right foot and bend right knee — your upper torso should now face the right side of the room, and your knees should be bent with body weight on the right foot (2); return arms to starting position as you step forward with left foot, keeping your toes slightly turned out (3); step right on the ball of your right foot, while pushing hands away to the sides in second position, shifting the weight to the right and bending the right knee (&); step about one foot to the left side with your left foot and bend left knee — your upper torso should now face the left side of the room, and your knees should be bent with body weight on the left foot (4). Begin again on the right, counting (5 & 6). Reverse beginning left, counting (7 & 8). Continue this exercise until it is smooth and comfortable. Remember, both knees must be bent by the time your feet are apart, and the body must go toward the foot that steps out last.

Step forward with your right foot.

Step left on the ball of your left foot, while pushing your arms out to the sides. Be sure to shift your weight to the left foot and to bend your left knee.

Step to the right so that the upper part of your body faces the right side of the room. When you've finished this step, be sure that your weight is now on your right foot.

GROOVIN'

BODY PLACEMENT:
Begin with your weight on the left foot, which should be slightly turned out. Place the toes of the right foot in back of the left heel. The right heel is off the floor. The arms hang loosely at the sides of the body.

MUSIC: Bounce tempo

COUNTS:
Use one count to step right. Use one count to raise left knee and snap fingers. Use one count to step left. Use one count to raise right knee. 1, 2, 3, 4. Repeat: 5, 6, 7, 8.

DESCRIPTION OF STEP:
Remember to keep your back straight during this exercise. You may want to snap your fingers or clap your hands each time you bounce. Step right foot forward about one foot (1); raise left foot off the floor so that your left heel comes next to the top of the right calf and bounce the right knee (2); step forward with the left foot and straighten the left leg as you step out on it—this will automatically straighten the right leg (3); raise right foot off the floor so that your right heel comes next to the top of left calf and bounce the left knee (4); step forward with right foot and straighten legs (5); raise left foot off floor with heel next to calf of right leg and bounce right knee (6); step forward with left foot and straighten legs (7); raise right foot off floor and bounce left knee (8). Continue to do this step until it becomes fun and feels right.

THE SWINGER

BODY PLACEMENT:
Begin with your weight on the right foot, which should be slightly turned out. Place the toes of the left foot in back of the right heel. The left heel is off the floor. Both knees are bent, and the arms and fingers are outstretched at shoulder level.

MUSIC: Bounce tempo

COUNTS:
Use one count to step left. Use the (&) count to kick right foot to right. Use one count to bring right foot to left knee. Use one count to step right foot back. Use one count to step left foot forward. Use one count to step right. Use the (&) count to kick left foot to left. Use one count to bring left foot to right knee. Use one count

to step left foot back and one count to step right foot forward.
1 & 2, 3, 4; 5 & 6, 7, 8.

Start from this position.

DESCRIPTION OF STEP:

Step left foot in front of your right foot, turning the left foot out slightly (1); keeping left knee bent, kick right foot to right side, straightening the right knee as you kick (&); keeping the left knee bent, bring right foot in next to the left knee and point the toes of the right foot to the floor (2); step ball of right foot directly in back of left foot, shifting weight to the right, and bend right knee so that both knees are now bent (3); step forward on left foot, transferring weight to left (4). Now you are ready to begin again: step right foot in front of left, turning out right foot slightly (5); keeping right knee bent, kick left foot to left side, straightening the left knee as you kick (&); keeping the right knee bent, bring left foot in next to right knee and point the toes of the left foot to the floor (6); step ball of left foot directly in back of right foot, shifting weight to the left, and bend left knee so that both knees are now bent (7); step forward on right foot, transferring weight to right (8). Continue to do this, starting on the opposite foot each time until you find it easy and comfortable for you.

Step on your left foot in front of your right foot. Be sure to turn the left foot out slightly.

Keeping your left knee slightly bent, kick your right foot
to your right side, straightening the right knee as you kick.

82

Keeping the left knee bent, bring your right foot up next to your
left knee, pointing the toes of your right foot toward the floor.

Step on the ball of your right foot behind your left foot, being sure to shift your weight to your right and to bend your right knee.

THE LATIN SWINGER

BODY PLACEMENT:
Begin with your weight on the right foot, which should be slightly turned out. Place the toes of the left foot in back of the right heel. The left heel is off the floor. Both knees are bent. Place both hands 2 inches in front of the stomach, with palms facing in and fingers outstretched. Arms form a diamond shape with elbows pointed.

MUSIC: Bounce tempo

COUNTS:
Use one count to step left. Use the (&) count to kick right foot to right. Use one count to bring right foot to left knee. Use one count to step right foot back. Use one count to step left foot forward. Use one count to step right. Use the (&) count to kick left foot to left. Use one count to bring left foot to right knee. Use one count to step left foot back and one count to step right foot forward.
1 & 2, 3, 4; 5 & 6, 7, 8.

DESCRIPTION OF STEP:
This is really the same as "The Swinger," but here it's done with an arm movement added. Step left foot in front of right, turning the left foot out slightly (1); keeping left knee bent, kick right foot to right side, straightening the right knee as you kick, and push hands and arms to the sides into second position (&); keeping the left knee bent, bring right foot in next to left knee and point the toes of the right foot to the floor while bringing the arms back to a diamond position (2); step ball of right foot directly in back of left foot, shifting weight to right, and bend right knee (3); step on left foot, transferring weight to the left (4); step right foot in front of left, turning right foot out slightly (5); keeping right knee bent, kick left foot to left side, straightening the left knee as you kick and pushing hands and arms to sides into second position (&); keeping the right knee bent, bring left foot in next to right knee and point the toes of the left foot to the floor while bringing the arms back to the diamond position (6); step ball of left foot directly in back of right foot, shifting weight to left, and bend left knee (7); step forward on right foot, transferring weight to the right (8). Continue doing this step until it is smooth and comfortable.

Start the step from this position.

Step on your left foot in front of your right foot,
turning your left foot out slightly.

Then, keeping your left knee slightly bent, kick your right foot
to your right side, straightening your right knee and pushing
your arms out to your sides as you kick.

Moving directly from the kick and keeping your left knee bent,
bring your right foot in next to your left knee, point your toes
toward the floor and bring your arms back to the diamond position.
Then continue as you did in The Swinger.

COMBINATIONS

COUNTER = BODY MOVEMENT

A counter-body movement is the use of one arm and shoulder with the opposite leg. For instance, you might put your right arm forward while pointing your left toe or your left arm forward while pointing your right toe.

BODY PLACEMENT:
Stand with the body facing front toward the mirror. Turn out the feet in the modified "V" position, with the heels touching. Arms hang loosely at your sides.

MUSIC: Medium tempo

COUNTS:
Use one count to slide right foot forward. Use one count to return right foot to "V" position and to bend both knees.
1, 2.
Use one count to slide left foot forward. Use one count to return left foot to "V" position and to bend both knees.
3, 4.
Repeat: 5, 6. Reverse: 7, 8.

DESCRIPTION OF STEP:
This exercise requires a smooth and continuous movement. Begin with the weight on your left foot. Slide the right foot forward as far as you can comfortably, and then point your toes on the right foot. As your right foot comes forward, your left arm moves forward and your right arm moves back (1). Now return the foot to the "V" position, bend both knees and bring arms back to the sides (2); shift the weight to the right foot, straightening knees, and slide the left foot forward as far as you can comfortably, then point the toes on the left foot. As your left foot comes forward, your right arm moves forward and your left arm moves back (3). Now return the left foot to the "V" position, bend both knees and bring arms back to the sides (4).

   Repeat entire exercise again, starting with the movement of the right foot (5); return to starting position or center (6); move left foot (7); back to center (8). Repeat the entire exercise, starting this time with the left foot pointing forward. Remember to use your stomach muscles at all times so that you will be able to retain your balance.

This photograph shows the second part of the Counter Body-Movement:
Slide your left foot forward as far as you can comfortably and point your toes, while swinging your right arm forward and your left arm back.

Move your left foot back to the starting position,
bend both knees and return your arms to your sides.

SIDE BY SIDE

BODY PLACEMENT:
Begin with your weight on the left foot, which should be slightly turned out. Place the ball of the right foot in back of the left heel. The right heel is off the floor. The arms hang loosely at the sides of the body.

MUSIC: Bounce tempo

COUNTS:
Use one count to step right. Use one count to step with left foot. Use one count to step right again and one count to step with left foot: 1, 2, 3, 4. Reverse, beginning left: 5, 6, 7, 8.

DESCRIPTION OF STEP:
Step right foot to right side (1); step left foot crossing in front of right (2); step right foot to right side again (3); now step ball of left foot in back of right, being sure to keep weight on right foot (4). Now reverse. Step left foot to left side (5); step right foot crossing in front of left (6); step left foot to left side again (7); now step ball of right foot in back of left, being sure to keep your weight on left foot (8). Repeat to right and then to left (1–8). Repeat and reverse several times until this step feels comfortable.

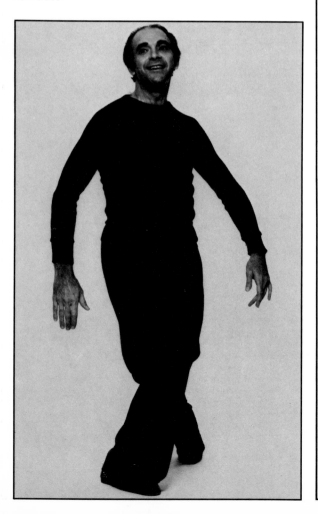

Start in this position—your weight should be on your left foot, your arms should hang loosely at the sides of your body, and your right foot should be behind your left foot. Remember to keep your right heel off the floor.

After you've done the step once, reverse the direction. Step on your left foot to your left side.

After you've repeated the side step, step on the ball of your right foot
in back of your left foot, being sure to keep your weight on your left foot.

THREE=STEP TURN

BODY PLACEMENT:
Begin with your weight on the left foot, which should be slightly turned out. Place the ball of the right foot in back of the left heel. The right heel is off the floor. Arms are out to the side in second position.

MUSIC: Bounce tempo

COUNTS:
Use one count to step right foot to right side. Use one count to step left foot crossing in front. Use one count to make one half-turn right. Use one count to step in back of right heel on ball of left foot.

1, 2, 3, 4. Reverse, beginning left: 5, 6, 7, 8.

DESCRIPTION OF STEP:
This is the same step used in "Side By Side," except that you will add a turn here. In order not to get dizzy or lose your balance while doing the turn, focus on an object at eye level in the direction in which you are turning. This practice, called "spotting," also makes your turns more consistent and precise. Step right foot to right side (1); cross left foot in front of right and pivot on the balls of both feet, as you turn your head and look to the right, until the front of your body faces the direction that your

Start in this position.

back did when you started. However, as your body turns, the head stays where it was when you started the turn, so that you should now be looking to the left side of your body (2). Step right foot to right side again, pivoting to the right, only this time your half-turn will bring you facing front (3). To complete the movement, step on the ball of your left foot in back of your right heel, but keep your weight on the right foot (4). Remember that you should be "spotting," so your head will be turning after your body does.

Step to your right with your right foot.

With your weight on the right foot, repeat to the left side. Step left foot to left side (5); cross right foot in front of left and pivot on the balls of both feet, as you turn your head and look to the left, until the front of your body faces the direction that your back did when you started. However, as your body turns, the head stays where it was when you started the turn, so that you should now be looking to the right (6). Step left foot to left side again, pivoting to the left, only this time your half-turn will bring you facing front (7). To complete the turn, step on the ball of your right foot in back of your left heel, but keep your weight on the left foot (8). Repeat and reverse several times until the turn is comfortable.

Pivot around, remembering to keep your head where it was when you started the turn.

THE DIPPER

BODY PLACEMENT:

Begin with your weight on the left foot, which should be slightly turned out. Place the ball of the right foot in back of the left heel. The right heel is off the floor. Both knees are bent, and the arms and fingers are outstretched at shoulder level in second position.

MUSIC: Bounce tempo

COUNTS:

Use one count to kick to right. Use one count to step back with right. Use one count to step to left side with left. Use one count to cross in front of left with right.

1, 2, 3, 4. Reverse, beginning left: 5, 6, 7, 8

DESCRIPTION OF STEP:

Kick right leg to right side, straightening both knees as you kick (1); moving directly from the

Moving from the starting position, kick your right leg to your right side while straightening both legs.

kick position, step the ball of your right foot in back of your left heel, making sure that both knees are bent again, and shifting weight to right foot (2); step left foot to left side (3); cross your right foot in front of left (4). Now begin to the left side: with weight on the right foot, kick your left leg to the left side, straightening both knees as you kick (5); moving directly from the kick position, step the ball of your left foot in back of your right heel, shifting weight to

As you bring your leg down from the kick, place the ball of your right foot in back of your left heel while bending both knees and shifting your weight to your right foot.

left foot (6); step right foot to right side (7); cross your left foot in front of right (8). There are two things to remember throughout this exercise: your arms are out to the sides in second position and the fingers are outstretched during entire combination, and your knees should be straight only during the kick. Keep repeating this until it feels comfortable.

After you've stepped your left foot to your left side, cross your right foot in front of your left.

THE SWIRL

BODY PLACEMENT:
Begin with your weight on the left foot, which should be slightly turned out. Place the ball of the right foot in back of the left heel. The right heel is off the floor. Both knees are bent. Arms and fingers are outstretched at shoulder level in second position.

MUSIC: Bounce tempo

COUNTS:
Use two counts to kick to right. Use two counts to step right foot back to begin turn. Use two counts to step left foot turning to left. Use two counts to step right foot to complete turn.
1, 2; 3, 4; 5, 6; 7, 8. Reverse, beginning left: 1, 2; 3, 4; 5, 6; 7, 8.

DESCRIPTION OF STEP:
"The Swirl" is like "The Dipper," except here you do the step with a turn. Kick right leg to right side, straightening both knees as you kick (1, 2); moving directly from the kick position, cross the ball of your right foot as far in back of your left heel as possible while pivoting on the balls of both feet until your body faces the back of the room—trying to keep your head facing to the front of the room as long as possible (3, 4); step left foot to left side (5, 6); step

Moving directly from your right kick, step on the ball of your right foot as far in back of your left heel as possible and begin to pivot toward your right.

the ball of your right foot in front of your left heel and pivot on the balls of both feet until you are facing the front once again (7, 8). If you turn properly, your weight should now be on the right foot, with the ball of the left foot directly behind the right heel, and both knees should be bent. Don't worry if your body seems to be on an angle—just straighten out your position so that you are facing front, and begin the combination starting to the left. You may find that you have to keep straightening out your body for a while until you become more proficient at the turns. With the weight on the right foot, kick the left leg to the left side, straightening both knees as you kick (1, 2); moving directly from the kick position, cross the ball of your left foot as far in back of your right heel as possible while pivoting on the balls of both feet until your body faces the back of the room—trying to keep your head facing to the front of the room (3, 4); step right foot to right side (5, 6); step the ball of your left foot in front of your right heel and pivot on the balls of both feet until you are facing the front of the room (7, 8). Keep practicing this combination both to the right and to the left, remembering to keep the knees bent, except when kicking, and the head as much to the front as possible.

Pivot on the balls of both feet until you're facing the back of the room.

TAKIN" OFF

BODY PLACEMENT:
The body faces the left corner of the room. Begin with the weight on the left foot, pointing front. Place the ball of the right foot in back of the left and bend both knees. Arms hang loosely at your sides.

MUSIC: Bounce tempo

COUNTS:
Use one count to kick right foot. Use the (&) count to step on ball of right foot to left heel. Use one count to step on left foot.
1 & 2. Repeat two times: 3 & 4, 5 & 6.
Use one count to cross front with right foot. Use the (&) count to step left foot to side. Use one count to step on right foot.
7 & 8.
1 & 2, 3 & 4, 5 & 6, 7 & 8. Reverse, beginning left: 1 & 2, 3 & 4, 5 & 6, 7 & 8.

This sequence shows the reverse of the step. After you've done the kick with your left foot, bend your left knee and step on the ball of your left foot behind your right heel.

Pick up your right foot and step on it

DESCRIPTION OF STEP:

Do a small kick with the right foot to the front of your body, straightening both knees as you kick. As you do the kick, turn your torso, shoulders and head toward your right side, while keeping the lower part of your body facing the left corner (1); bend right knee and step on ball of right foot next to left heel while bringing the torso, shoulders and head back to face the front (&). Your weight should now be on the ball of the right foot. Pick up the left foot and step down on it (2). Repeat: Kick right (3); step on ball of right foot (&); step on left foot (4). Repeat again (5, &, 6). Put your arms out to the sides in second position, and cross your right foot in front of your left (7); step on ball of left foot to left side while turning your body to the right corner of the room

Put your arms out to your sides and cross your left foot in front of your right foot.

(&); step again on right foot (8). Weight should now be on the right foot, with the ball of the left foot touching the floor so that you can begin the entire step once again, from your original position. This time, start by doing a small kick with the left foot to the front of your body, straightening both knees as you kick. As you do the kick, turn your torso, shoulders and head toward your left side while keeping

Step on the ball of your right foot to the right side while turning your body toward the left.

the lower part of your body facing the right corner (1); bend left knee and step on ball of left foot next to the right heel while bringing the torso, shoulders and head back to face the front (&). Your weight should now be on the ball of the left foot. Pick up the right foot and step on it (2). Repeat: Kick left (3); step on ball of left foot (&); step on right foot (4). Repeat again (5, &, 6). Put your arms out to the sides in second position, and cross your left foot in front of your right (7); step on ball of right foot to right side while turning your body to the left corner of the room (&); step again on left foot (8).

Step again on your left foot.

TAKIN' OFF AND COMIN' DOWN

BODY PLACEMENT:
The body faces the left corner of the room. Begin with the weight on the left foot, pointing front. Place the ball of the right foot in back of the left heel and bend both knees. Arms hang loosely at your sides.

MUSIC: Bounce tempo

COUNTS:
Use one count to kick right. Use the (&) count to step on ball of right foot. Use one count to step on left foot. Use one count to cross right foot in front of left. Use the (&) count to step to left side on left foot. Use one count to step on right foot.
1 & 2, 3 & 4. Reverse, beginning left: 5 & 6, 7 & 8.

DESCRIPTION OF STEP:
Do a small kick with the right foot while turning the top of your body to the right side (1); step on ball of right foot next to left heel while returning the top of your body to its original position (&); pick up left foot and step down on it (2); put arms out to the sides in second position and cross right foot in front of left (3); step ball of left foot to left side while turning body to right corner of room (&); step again on right foot (4); with weight on right foot, kick left foot (5); step on ball of left foot next to right heel (&); pick up right foot and step down on it (6); cross left foot in front of right (7); step ball of right foot to right side, turning body to left corner of room (&); step again on left (8). Continue this step until it becomes comfortable.

TAKIN" OFF PLUS THREE

BODY PLACEMENT:
The body faces the left corner of the room. Begin with the weight on the left foot, pointing front. Place the ball of the right foot in back of the left heel and bend both knees. Arms hang loosely at your sides.

MUSIC: Bounce tempo

COUNTS:
Use one count to kick right. Use the (&) count to step on ball of right foot. Use one count to step on left foot. Use one count to cross right foot in front of left. Use the (&) count to step to left side on left foot. Use one count to step on right foot.
1 & 2, 3 & 4. Repeat the steps you did on counts 3 & 4, beginning *left* for counts 5 & 6, and beginning *right* for 7 & 8. Reverse, beginning left: 1 & 2, 3 & 4, 5 & 6, 7 & 8.

DESCRIPTION OF STEP:
Do a small kick with right foot (1); step on ball of right foot to side of left heel (&); pick up left foot and step down on it (2); put arms out to sides in second position and cross right foot in front of left (3); step on ball of left foot to left side while turning body to right corner (&); step again on right foot (4); cross left foot in front of right (5); step on ball of right foot to right side while turning body to left corner (&); step again on left foot (6); cross right foot in front of left (7); step on ball of left foot to left side while turning body to right corner (&); step again on right foot (8). Now you have your weight on the right, so you can begin the entire combination again—starting with the kick on the left foot. Kick with left foot (1); step on ball of left foot to side of right heel (&); pick up right foot and step down on it (2); put arms out to the side in second position and cross left foot in front of right (3); step on ball of right foot to right side while turning body to left corner (&); step again on left foot (4); cross right foot in front of left (5); step on ball of left foot to left side while turning body to right corner (&); step again on right foot (6); cross left foot in front of right (7); step on ball of right foot to right side while turning body to left corner (&); step again on left foot (8). Continue to do this combination on both sides until you feel comfortable with it.

STEP AND ARISE

BODY PLACEMENT:
Begin with your weight on the left foot, slightly turned out. Place the toes of the right foot in back of the left heel. The right heel is off the floor. Arms hang loosely at the sides of the body.

MUSIC: Fast tempo

COUNTS:
Use three counts to step and one count to rise up on the ball of the foot.
1, 2, 3, 4; 5, 6, 7, 8.

DESCRIPTION OF STEP:
Step right foot forward (1); step left foot forward (2); step right foot forward (3); rise up on ball of right foot while picking up left foot and

raising left knee to place left foot behind right knee, toes pointing downward. At the same time, the right arm moves naturally forward and extends at shoulder level, while the left arm moves naturally back to extend at shoulder level, so that the upper torso faces the left corner of the room (4). Reverse: Step left foot forward (5); step right foot forward (6); step left foot forward (7); rise up on ball of left foot while picking up right foot and raising right knee to place right foot behind left knee, toes pointing downward. At the same time, the left arm moves naturally forward and extends at shoulder level, while the right arm moves naturally back to extend at shoulder level, so that the upper torso faces the right corner of the room (8). Repeat this step many times until it feels comfortable.

STEP AND JUMP

BODY PLACEMENT:
Begin with your weight on the left foot, slightly turned out. Place the toes of the right foot in back of the left heel. The right heel is off the floor. Arms hang loosely at the sides of the body.

MUSIC: Fast tempo

COUNTS:
Use three counts to step. Use the (&) count to jump upward. Use one count to land.
1, 2, 3 & 4; 5, 6, 7 & 8.

DESCRIPTION OF STEP:
Step right foot forward (1); step left foot forward (2); step right foot forward (3); pick up left foot and raise left knee to place left foot behind right knee, toes pointing downward, as you jump upward. At the same time, the right arm moves naturally forward and extends at shoulder level, while the left arm moves naturally back to extend at shoulder level, so that the upper torso faces the left corner of the room (&); remaining in this position, land on right foot (4). Reverse: Step left foot forward (5); step right foot forward (6); step left foot forward (7); pick up right foot and raise right knee to place right foot behind left knee, toes pointing downward, as you jump upward. At the same time, the left arm moves naturally forward and extends at shoulder level, while the right arm moves naturally back to extend at shoulder level, so that the upper torso faces the right corner of the room (&); remaining in this position, land on left foot (8). Repeat this step many times until it feels comfortable.

THE LINDY

BODY PLACEMENT:
The body faces front. The weight is on the left foot, pointing forward. Place the ball of the right foot behind the left heel. The right heel is off the floor. Bend both knees. Arms hang loosely at your sides.

MUSIC: Bright and Bouncy tempo

COUNTS:
Use one count to step right foot to right side. Use the (&) count to slide left foot. Use one count to step right foot to right side. Use one count to step on ball of left foot behind right. Use one count to step right foot to right.
1 & 2, 3, 4. Reverse, beginning left: 5 & 6, 7, 8.

Moving from the starting position, move your right foot about 12 inches to your right side.

DESCRIPTION OF STEP:

Step about 12 inches to the right side with the right foot (1); slide left foot next to right (&); step about 12 inches further to right side with the right foot (2); step on ball of left foot behind right foot while putting your arms out to the sides and turning your legs, upper torso and head to face right corner of room (3); step right foot to right front while turning your legs, upper torso and head to front (4). Your entire body should now be facing front, and your arms should once again be at your sides.

DESCRIPTION OF STEP:

Quickly slide your left foot next to your right foot.

We will now reverse the step, starting to the left. Step about 12 inches to left side with left foot (5); slide right foot next to left (&); step about 12 inches further to left side with left foot (6); step on ball of right foot behind left foot while putting your arms out to the sides and turning your legs, upper torso and head to face left corner of room (7); step left foot to left front while turning your legs, upper torso and head to front (8). Continue to do this step, first going to the right and then to the left, until it is comfortable. Remember to keep your knees bent throughout.

Step on the ball of your left foot behind your right foot while raising your arms to shoulder level and turning your body toward the right corner of the room.

Just before returning your arms to your sides, step on
your right foot and turn your entire body toward the front.

THE LINDY STEPS OUT

BODY PLACEMENT:
The body faces front. The weight is on the left foot, pointing forward. Place the ball of the right foot behind the left heel. The right heel is off the floor. Bend both knees. Arms hang loosely at your sides.

MUSIC: Bright and Bouncy tempo

COUNTS:
Use one count to step right foot to right side. Use the (&) count to slide left foot. Use one count to step right foot to right side. Use one count to step back on ball of left foot. Use one count to step right with right foot.
1 & 2, 3, 4.
Use one count to kick left. Use the (&) count to step on ball of left foot. Use one count to step on right foot. Use one count to step left. Use one count to step right foot in front of left foot.
5 & 6, 7, 8.
Reverse, beginning left: 1 & 2, 3, 4; 5 & 6, 7, 8.

After you've completed the basic Lindy step, kick your left foot to the left while turning the top part of your body toward the left corner of the room.

DESCRIPTION OF STEP:

Step about 12 inches to right side with right foot (1); slide left foot next to right foot (&); step about 12 inches further to right side with right foot (2); step on ball of left foot behind right foot—shifting weight to left foot—while putting the arms into second position and turning the legs, upper torso and head to face the right corner of the room (3); step right foot to right front while turning your legs, upper torso and head back to the front, returning your arms to your sides and bending both knees (4); do a small kick to the left with the left foot while straightening both knees and turning the torso, head and shoulders toward the left corner of the room (5); moving directly from this kick position, bend left

Moving directly from the kick, bend your left knee and step on the ball of your left foot to the side of your right heel while turning the top part of your body back to the front of the room.

knee and step on ball of left foot to side of right heel—shifting weight to left—while turning the torso, shoulders and head back to the front (&); step on right foot (6); pick up left foot and place it down with toes pointing toward the left corner of the room (7); cross right foot in front of left while twisting ball of left foot so that both hips are facing the front of the room (8). Reverse entire step. Step about 12 inches to left side with left foot (1); slide right foot next to left foot (&); step about 12 inches more to left side with left foot (2); step on ball of right foot behind left foot—shifting weight to right foot—while putting the arms into second position and turning the legs, upper torso and head to face the left corner of the room (3); step left foot

After you've stepped on your right foot, place your left foot, with toes pointing downward, toward the left corner of the room.

to left front while turning your legs, upper torso and head back to the front, returning your arms to your sides and bending both knees (4); do a small kick to the right with the right foot while straightening both knees and turning the torso, head and shoulders toward the right corner of the room (5); moving directly from this kick position, bend right knee and step on ball of right foot to side of left heel—shifting weight to right—while turning the torso, shoulders and head back to the front (&); step on left foot (6); pick up right foot and place it down with toes pointing toward the right corner of the room (7); cross left foot in front of right while twisting ball of right foot so that both hips are facing the front of the room (8).

Cross your right foot in front of your left foot while twisting on the ball of your left foot so that you're now facing the front of the room.

A JAZZ ROUTINE: "EASE ON DOWN THE ROAD"

"Ease On Down the Road"
Recorded on Atlantic Records, #SD18137
From the original soundtrack of the
Broadway musical *The Wiz*

Introduction:
Wait offstage during the instrumental introduction that precedes the vocal entrance.

BACKSTAGE

UP

RIGHT   CENTER   LEFT

DOWN

AUDIENCE

STEP 1: "EASIN" ON DOWN"

(Come on,) ease on down, ease on down the road.

Begin Step 1 on the vocal entrance. Note that the downbeat, the beat on which you start dancing, comes on the word "ease." Enter from upstage right, diagonally, with your body facing downstage left.

Step Right foot forward (1); Step Left foot quickly to the side of Right foot (&); Step Right foot forward again (2); Step Left foot forward (3); Step Right foot forward (4).

Now REPEAT the above steps, beginning with your Left foot, for counts (5 & 6, 7, 8).

(Come on,) ease on down, ease on down the road.

The next eight counts are also done on the diagonal. Step Right foot to the side, keeping feet parallel (1); Cross Left foot in front of Right foot (2); Step Right foot to the side, keeping feet parallel (3); Place ball of Left foot in back of Right, keeping the Left heel off the floor so that the body weight remains on the Right foot (4).

REVERSE the last four counts, beginning on the Left foot, for counts (5, 6, 7, 8).

(Don't you) carry nothin' that might be a load. Come on, ease on down, ease on down the road.

On the next sixteen counts, turn your body so that it faces downstage. Step Right foot quickly to right side (&); Step Left foot quickly in place (1); place ball of Right foot beside Left foot, keeping weight on Left foot, in preparation for beginning this step again (2). Step Right foot quickly to right side again (&); Step Left foot quickly in place (3); Step Right foot next to Left, shifting the body weight to Right foot, leaving Left foot free to reverse entire step (4).

REVERSE above, beginning on the Left foot, for counts (& 5, 6, &, 7, 8).

Cross Right foot in front of Left (1); Touch ball of Left foot to left side, keeping weight on Right foot (2); Cross Left foot in front of Right (3); Touch ball of Right foot to right side, keeping weight on Left foot (4).

Step Right foot quickly in back of Left heel (5); Step Left foot quickly to left side (&); Cross Right foot in front of Left foot (6); Step Left foot to left side (7); Step Right foot next to Left foot, shifting weight to Right foot to leave Left foot free (8).

You have completed Step 1 in four sets of eight counts, or eight measures.

STEP 2:

(Come on,) ease on down, ease on down the road.
(Come on,) ease on down, ease on down the road.
(Don't you) carry nothin' that might be a load.
Come on, ease on down, ease on down the road.

REPEAT STEP 1, beginning with the Left foot. This time the body is facing downstage, and you should move from right to left in the downstage area. Again, you should complete four sets of eight counts, or a total of eight more measures.

STEP 3:

Pick your right foot up, when your left one's down.

Pause two counts, with weight still on Left foot (1, 2); Raise Right knee, lifting Right foot off floor and pointing toes downward while turning upper torso to face right (3); Put Right foot down (4); Step Left foot quickly to the side while turning body to face right (&); Step Right foot quickly in place, so that both feet are now facing downstage right (5); Raise Left knee, lifting Left foot off the floor and pointing the toes downward (6); Place ball of Left foot to the side, parallel to the Right foot (7); Pause, being sure to keep weight on the Right foot (8).

Come on, make your feet keep movin', don't you lose your ground.

Beginning with the Left foot, walk to upstage right, clockwise in a large circle for eight counts: Left (1); Right (2); Left (3); Right (4); Left (5); Right (6); Left (7); Right (8).

During the next eight counts, your body will be facing left downstage, and you should move in that direction.

'Cause the road you're walking might be long sometime,
But you just keep stepping and you'll be just fine.
"WALKING CHA-CHA":

Step Left foot forward (1); Pause (2); Step Right foot forward (3); Pause (4); Step Left foot forward (5); Right foot forward (6); Left foot forward (7); Step with Right foot, pivoting your body to the left so that you have turned around completely and are now facing the upstage right corner (8). For the next eight counts you will be moving upstage right until you reach center stage.

Step Left foot forward (1); Pause (2); Step Right foot forward (3); Pause (4); Step Left foot forward (5); Right foot forward (6); Pivot on ball of Left foot, turning your body to the right until you are facing downstage, while picking up the Right foot (7); step forward, bending both knees into a demi-plié (8).

You have completed Step 3 in four sets of eight counts, which is equal to another eight measures.

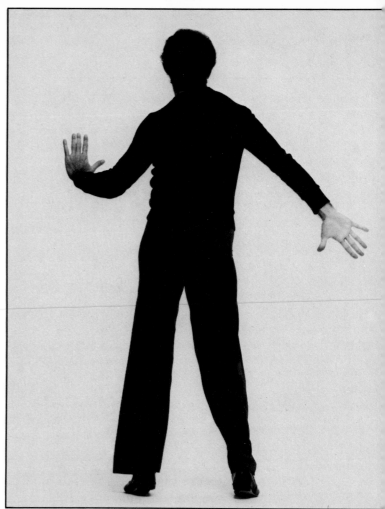

STEP 4:

(Come on,) ease on down, ease on down the road.

Hold demi-plié from preceding step for three counts (1, 2, 3); Raise Left knee, lifting Left foot off floor, pointing toes downward (4); Step Left foot forward (5); Step Right foot next to left (6); Step Left foot to left side (7); Bend Right knee, transferring weight to Right (8).

(Come on,) ease on down, ease on down the road.

Step ball of Left foot in back of Right foot into demi-plié (1); Pause (2, 3); Pick up Left knee, lifting Left foot off floor, pointing toes downward (4); Step Left foot forward (5); Step Right foot next to Left (6); Step Left foot to left side (7); Bend Right knee, transferring weight to Right (8).

(Don't you) carry nothin' that might be a load.
Come on, ease on down, ease on down the road.
"WALKING CHA-CHA":
Step Left foot forward, moving to left downstage (1); Pause (2); Step Right foot forward (3); Pause (4); Step Left foot forward (5); Right Foot forward (6); Step with Left foot—at the same time picking up Right knee, lifting Right foot off floor, pointing toes downward—pivoting your body to the right so that you have turned around completely and are now facing the upstage right corner (7, 8). For the next eight counts you will be moving upstage right until you reach center stage.

Step on Ball of Right foot in back of Left foot (&); Step on Left foot (1); Step Right foot forward (2); Pause (3); Step Left foot forward (4); Step on Ball of Right foot (&); Step on Left foot (5); Step Right foot forward (6); Step Left foot forward and pivot to right, turning downstage (7); Step Right foot forward (8).

You have now completed another four sets of eight counts, or eight measures.

STEP 5:

'Cause there may be times when you wish you wasn't born.

You are now standing center stage, with your body facing downstage. Cross Left foot in front of Right foot (1); Kick Right foot forward (2); Step Right foot way in back of Left foot (3); Keeping weight on right foot, step on ball of Left foot, crossing in back of Right foot (4). These steps are the "Charleston." It may be before your time!) Touch left heel forward, still with weight on Right foot (5); Step Left foot forward (6); Touch Right heel forward, keeping weight on Left foot (7); Step Right foot forward (8).

'Cause you wake one mornin' and you'll find your courage gone.
But just know that feelin' only lasts a little while.

REPEAT above "Charleston Step" two more times for counts (1–8, 1–8).

You just stick with us and we'll show you how to smile.

Travel to left side while body faces front, beginning by stepping Left foot to left side (1); Cross Right foot in front of Left foot (2); Step Left foot to left side (3); Step Right quickly (&); Touch ball of Left foot to left side, keeping weight on Right foot (4); Step Left foot to left side (5); Cross Right foot in front of Left foot (6); Step Left foot to left side again (7); Step Right foot quickly to left (&); Step Left foot to left side again, shifting weight to Left foot (8).

You have now completed another four sets of eight counts, which equals eight measures.

STEP 6:

(Come on,) ease on down, ease on down the road.
(Come on,) ease on down, ease on down the road.
(Don't you) carry nothin' that might be a load.
Come on, ease on down, ease on down the . . .

Now go back to the beginning of the dance routine. Repeat all of Step 1, beginning on the Right foot, but omitting the last four counts (5–8). Proceed directly to the following Interlude.

INTERLUDE:
Step Right foot to right side, bending both knees, while lifting Left heel off the floor, remembering to keep weight on the Right foot (1); Pause (2, 3); Pivot on ball of Right foot, lifting up Left knee, turning left to face the opposite direction, upstage (4); Cross Left foot in front of Right foot (5); Cross Right foot in front of Left foot (6); Step Left foot to left side, shifting weight to Left foot (7); Turn head sharply over Right shoulder to face downstage (8).

Walk upstage Right (1); Left (2); Right (3); Left (4); Right (5); Step Left foot while turning body to right (6); Leap with Right foot to right side, at the same doing a small kick with the Left foot (7); Leap with Left foot to left side, at the same time doing a small kick with the Right foot (8).

STEP 7:

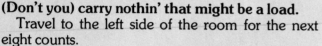

This is the last step of your dance routine. You are going to repeat the first eight counts of the first step of your routine—"Easin' On Down"—six times, following these stage directions:

(Come on,) ease on down, ease on down the road.
  Travel downstage center for the first eight counts.

(Come on,) ease on down, ease on down the road.
  Travel to the right side of the room for the next eight counts.

(Don't you) carry nothin' that might be a load.
  Travel to the left side of the room for the next eight counts.

Come on, ease on down, ease on down the road.
Come on, ease on down, ease on down the road.
Come on, ease on down, ease on down the road.

Turn your body to face the right diagonal corner upstage and continue to do this step to exit as the music fades.

SUGGESTED RECORDS

Dr. Buzzard's Original Savannah Band

RCA Records, #APL1-1504

Side #1: Band #3 — Bright and Bouncy tempo
Side #2: Band #2 — Bounce tempo
Band #3 — Bounce tempo

The Hungry Years, Neil Sedaka

MCA Records, #PIG-2157 (MCA-838)

Side #1: Band #2 — Slow tempo
Side #2: Band #1 — Bright and Bouncy tempo
Band #4 — Slow and Dreamy tempo
Band #5 — Slow and Dreamy tempo

Sound of a Drum, Ralph MacDonald

Marlin Records, #2202

Side #1: Band #1 — Slow Percussion tempo
Side #2: Band #3 — Medium Percussion tempo

Let's Get It Together, El Coco

AVI Records, #AVL-6006

Side #1: Band #3 — Medium tempo
Side #2: Band #1 — Medium tempo
Band #4 — Bounce tempo

Down to Love Town, The Originals

Soul Records, #S6-749s1

Side #2: Band #3 — Slow tempo

Rocky Road, The New Ventures

United Artists Records, #UA-LA586-G

Side #1: Band #1 — Bounce tempo
Band #2 — Bright tempo
Side #2: Band #2 — Slow tempo
Band #3 — Bright and Bouncy tempo

Trying to Get the Feeling, Barry Manilow

Artista Records, #A14060-SB

Side #1: Band #1 — Slow tempo
Band #2 — Bright tempo

They Said It Couldn't Be Done, The Dells

Mercury Records, SRM 1-1145

Side #2: Band #1 — Medium tempo

The Ritchie Family African Queens

Marlin Records, #2206

Side #2: Band #2 — Slow Percussion tempo

Eddie Drennon and the B.B.S. Unltd

Casablanca Records, #NBLP-7062-BS

Side #1: Band #1 — Slow Percussion tempo
Band #2 — Slow Percussion tempo
Band #3 — Slow Percussion tempo
Side #2: Band #1 — Bounce tempo

Light of Worlds, Kool and the Gang

De-Lite Records, #DEP-2014-B

Side #1: Band #1 — Medium tempo
Side #2: Band #4 — Slow tempo

Sweet Beginnings, Marlena Shaw

Columbia Records, #PC-34458

Side #1: Band #1 — Bounce tempo
Band #4 — Bright and Bouncy tempo
Side #2: Band #3 — Medium tempo

Devil's Gun, C.J. and Co.

Westbound Records, #WB-301

Side #1: Band #1 — Fast tempo
Side #2: Band #2 — Fast tempo
Band #1 — Medium tempo

Songs in the Key of Life, Stevie Wonder

Tamla Records, #TI3-340C2

Side #1: Band #5 — Medium tempo — strong beat
Side #2: Band #1 — Medium tempo — strong beat

CeliBee and the Buzzy Bunch

APA Records, #LP-77001

Side #1: Band #1 — Fast tempo
Band #3 — Slow and Dreamy tempo
Side #2: Band #3 — Medium Percussion tempo

The Wiz

Atlantic Records, #SD-18137

Side #1: Band #2 — Fast tempo
Band #3 — Medium tempo
Side #2: Band #7 — Slow and Dreamy tempo

Gonna Fly Now, Theme from *Rocky*

United Artists Records, #UA-XW940-Y

Four Seasons of Love, Donna Summer

Casablanca Records, #NBLP-7038

Side #1: Band #1—Fast tempo
Side #2: Band #1—Medium tempo
            Band #2—Slow tempo

Village People

Casablanca Records, #NBLP-7064

Side #1: All Bands—Fast tempo
Side #2: Band #2—Medium tempo

Cosmic Wind, Mike Theodore Orchestra

Westbound Records, #WB-305

Side #1: Band #2—Easy, with a beat tempo
            Band #3—Medium tempo
Side #2: Band #1—Fast tempo

Je t'aime, St. Tropez

Butterfly Records

Side #1: Band #2—Slow tempo

El Coco Cocomotion

AVL Records, #AVL-6012

Side #1: Band #1—Fast tempo
Side #2: Band #1—Medium with Bounce tempo
            Band #3—Medium with Bounce tempo

What Color Is Love, Dee Dee Sharp Gamble

Philadelphia International Records, #PZ-34437

Side #1: Band #1—Slow and Bluesy tempo
Side #2: Band #4—Bright and Bouncy tempo

Saturday Night Fever (Original sound track)

RSO Records
All bands—Various tempos

Romeo and Juliet

Casablanca Records, #NBLP-7086

Side #1: All bands—Fast tempo

Bionic Boogie

Polydor Records, #PD1-6123

Side #1: All bands—Various tempos
Side #2: All bands—Various tempos

Tuxedo Junction

Butterfly Records, #Fly 007

Side #1: Band #1—Bright and Bouncy tempo
Side #2: Band #3—Easy, with a beat

ABOUT THE AUTHOR

ROBERT AUDY, author of *Tap Dancing,* received most of his dance training from Ollie Wood and Alyce Hogan in Grand Rapids, Michigan, where he also gained his first experience as a dance teacher. Prompted by his teachers to pursue a career as a professional dancer, he came to New York City to study with the great masters of dance and to make his mark in the dance world. He studied ballet with Madame Fedorava Fokine, Mia Slavinska and Francis Cole; primitive and modern dance with Sevilla Fort and Jane Dodge, and tap with Paul Draper, Roye Dodge, Ernest Carlos, Dave Morganstern and Francis Cole.

After a brief career as a professional dancer, Mr. Audy realized that he wanted to choreograph and to teach artists how to perform, rather than to perform himself. His reputation as a dancer grew, and he began to teach master classes for dancing schools and universities throughout the United States. Mr. Audy's tap and jazz technique is now used by leading teachers throughout the world. In fact, Mr. Audy is credited with being the first dancer to organize jazz movements so that they could be taught to the dancer who was not classically trained.

Among his credits as a director and choreographer are over one hundred musicals for theaters across the country, including productions of *No, No, Nanette* with Vicki Lawrence and Gale Gordon; *Funny Girl* with Carol Lawrence; *George M* with Joel Grey; *Music Man* with Peter Marshall; and *My Fair Lady* with Jane Powell.

Some of the artists who have studied under or who have been coached by Mr. Audy are Shirley MacLaine, Ben Vereen, Joel Grey, Diane Keaton, Madeline Kahn, Celeste Holm, Cybill Shepherd, James Taylor, Jennifer O'Neil, Jerry Orbach, Lorna Luft and Tita (Mrs. Sammy) Cahn.

In theatrical circles, Mr. Audy is known as the "tap dancer's tap dancer."

Also by Robert Audy:

Tap Dancing: How to Teach Yourself to Tap

JAZZ DANCING